A Brief History of

Portugal

Crafted by Skriuwer

Table of Contents

Introduction

Overview of Portugal's Significance in World History
Portugal, a small nation located on the westernmost edge of
Europe, has played a significant role in shaping world history
through its exploration, colonization, and cultural contributions.
Despite its size, Portugal's impact on the world has been immense
and far-reaching.

One of the key aspects of Portugal's significance in world history
is its role as a pioneer in the Age of Exploration. During the 15th
and 16th centuries, Portuguese navigators embarked on daring
voyages of discovery, seeking new trade routes to Asia and
Africa. Led by figures such as Prince Henry the Navigator, Vasco
da Gama, and Bartolomeu Dias, Portuguese sailors traveled to
distant lands, opening up new trade routes and establishing a
vast overseas empire.

Portugal's maritime discoveries had profound implications for
global trade and geopolitics. The establishment of trade networks
with Africa, Asia, and the Americas brought wealth and resources
to Portugal and fueled the growth of its empire. Portuguese
explorers were among the first Europeans to reach India, China,
and Japan, paving the way for the era of European colonialism
and shaping the course of world history.

Portugal's colonial empire, which spanned continents and
encompassed diverse cultures, had a lasting impact on the
regions it controlled. Portuguese colonization brought new crops,
technologies, and languages to distant lands, while also imposing
European customs and institutions. The legacy of Portuguese

colonialism can still be seen today in the language, culture, and heritage of countries in Africa, Asia, and the Americas.

In addition to its role as a colonial power, Portugal has made significant cultural and intellectual contributions to the world. The Portuguese language, with its rich literary tradition and global reach, is spoken by millions of people around the world and serves as a bridge between different cultures and nations. Portuguese explorers and scholars made important contributions to the fields of cartography, navigation, and natural history, expanding European knowledge of the world and shaping the development of science and exploration.

Furthermore, Portugal's history is marked by periods of political and social change that have had reverberations beyond its borders. From the Christian Reconquista against Moorish rule to the Carnation Revolution that brought an end to the Estado Novo dictatorship, Portugal's struggles for independence, democracy, and social justice have inspired movements and revolutions around the world.

In conclusion, Portugal's significance in world history lies in its role as a pioneer of exploration, a colonial power, a cultural influencer, and a symbol of resilience and change. Despite its size, Portugal has left a lasting imprint on the global stage, shaping the course of world events and contributing to the richness and diversity of human civilization.

Purpose and scope of the book
The purpose and scope of the book "The History of Portugal" is to provide a comprehensive and detailed account of Portugal's rich and diverse historical journey from ancient times to the modern era. Through its detailed chapters, the book aims to offer readers

a thorough understanding of the key events, figures, and developments that have shaped Portugal's history and its significance in the world.

The book begins with an Introduction that sets the stage by highlighting Portugal's importance in global history. It outlines the country's contributions to world exploration, trade, and culture, emphasizing its role as a key player in the Age of Discovery and the establishment of a vast colonial empire. The introduction also introduces the purpose and structure of the book, providing readers with a roadmap of the chapters to come.

Chapter 1 delves into Ancient Portugal, exploring the prehistoric and early human settlements that laid the foundation for the region's development. It examines the influence of Iberian tribes and Celts, as well as the impact of Phoenician, Greek, and Carthaginian civilizations on Portugal's early history.

Subsequent chapters cover key periods in Portugal's history, including the Roman conquest and integration of Lusitania (Chapter 2), the Islamic period and the emergence of Portuguese identity (Chapter 3), the birth of Portugal as an independent nation (Chapter 4), and the Age of Expansion that saw Portugal establish a global empire (Chapter 5).

The book also delves into the Golden Age of Portugal, a period of power and wealth marked by significant cultural and scientific achievements (Chapter 6). It explores the Iberian Union and the subsequent restoration of Portuguese independence (Chapter 7), as well as the Enlightenment and Reform era marked by modernization efforts and social changes (Chapter 8).
Moving into more recent history, the book covers the turbulent 19th century marked by political instability and social change

(Chapter 9), the establishment of the First Republic and Portugal's role in World War I (Chapter 10), and the rise of the Estado Novo regime under Salazar (Chapter 11).

The book also delves into the Carnation Revolution and the transition to democracy (Chapter 12), as well as contemporary Portugal's integration into the European Union and its economic challenges in the late 20th and early 21st centuries (Chapter 13).

In its conclusion, the book provides a summary of Portugal's historical journey, reflecting on its national identity and offering insights into its future prospects. The appendices offer additional resources, including a timeline of key events, biographies of notable figures, a glossary of terms, and suggestions for further reading.

Overall, "The History of Portugal" aims to be a comprehensive and informative resource for readers interested in delving into the complexities and nuances of Portugal's historical narrative, highlighting its impact on the world stage and its enduring cultural legacy.

Chapter 1

Ancient Portugal

Prehistoric and early human settlements
Prehistoric and early human settlements in Portugal provide a fascinating insight into the ancient history and cultural development of the region. This period lays the foundation for understanding the complexities of Portugal's rich historical journey.

The earliest evidence of human presence in Portugal dates back to the Paleolithic era, around 500,000 years ago. Stone tools and artifacts found in caves and open-air sites indicate that early humans inhabited the region, hunting wild animals and gathering food. The natural resources and favorable climate of Portugal would have made it an attractive area for early human settlement.

During the Neolithic period, around 5,000 to 4,000 BC, farming and animal domestication practices spread in Portugal, leading to the establishment of permanent settlements. Communities started to engage in agriculture, pottery-making, and weaving, marking a shift towards a more sedentary lifestyle. Megalithic structures, such as dolmens and menhirs, were erected during this period, serving as burial sites or religious monuments, reflecting the spiritual beliefs of the Neolithic inhabitants.

The Bronze Age, from around 2,000 to 800 BC, witnessed the introduction of metalworking technologies in Portugal, leading to the production of bronze tools and weapons. Trade networks expanded, connecting Portugal to other Mediterranean cultures, and influencing the local material culture and social structures. Hillforts, fortified settlements located on hilltops or promontories, became common during this period, serving as centers of power and defense.

The Iron Age, from around 800 BC to the Roman conquest, saw the emergence of distinct regional cultures in Portugal. The influence of Iberian tribes, such as the Lusitanians, Celtici, and Vettones, shaped the socio-political landscape of the region. These tribes practiced agriculture, animal husbandry, and metalworking, and engaged in trade with neighboring cultures. Hillforts expanded in size and complexity, indicating social stratification and organized warfare.

The arrival of Mediterranean civilizations, such as the Phoenicians, Greeks, and Carthaginians, introduced new technologies, trade goods, and cultural influences to Portugal. Phoenician and Carthaginian trading posts were established along the coast, facilitating the exchange of goods and ideas between the indigenous populations and the Mediterranean world. Greek colonies, such as Olisipo (modern-day Lisbon), played a significant role in the commercial and cultural interactions between Portugal and the Mediterranean civilizations.

In conclusion, the prehistoric and early human settlements in Portugal laid the groundwork for the development of complex societies and cultural exchanges in the region. The diverse archaeological evidence from this period provides valuable insights into the lifestyles, beliefs, and interactions of the ancient inhabitants of Portugal. Understanding this foundational period is crucial for appreciating the historical trajectory of Portugal and its significance in the broader context of world history.

The influence of Iberian tribes and the Celts

The influence of Iberian tribes and the Celts in ancient Portugal played a significant role in shaping the region's cultural and historical development. During ancient times, the Iberian Peninsula was inhabited by various indigenous tribes with distinct languages, customs, and social structures. These tribes had a profound impact on the early history of Portugal, particularly in the pre-Roman period.

The Iberian tribes were known for their advanced agricultural practices, skilled craftsmanship, and complex social hierarchies. They established fortified settlements and engaged in trade with other Mediterranean cultures, such as the Phoenicians and Greeks. The Iberians also developed a unique artistic style characterized by intricate metalwork, pottery, and sculpture.

One of the most notable influences on ancient Portugal was the arrival of the Celts, a group of Indo-European peoples who migrated to the Iberian Peninsula around the 1st millennium BCE. The Celts brought with them their distinctive language, beliefs, and material culture, which blended with the existing Iberian traditions to create a diverse and dynamic cultural landscape.

The Celts introduced new technologies, such as ironworking and chariot warfare, which revolutionized the way of life in ancient Portugal. They also had a profound impact on the region's religious beliefs and practices, with the introduction of Celtic deities and rituals that coexisted alongside the native Iberian spiritual traditions.

The interaction between the Iberian tribes and the Celts resulted in cultural exchange, intermarriage, and the emergence of hybrid societies that combined elements of both cultures. This cultural fusion enriched the artistic, linguistic, and social fabric of ancient Portugal, laying the foundation for the diverse and cosmopolitan society that would later emerge in the region.

The presence of the Iberian tribes and the Celts also influenced the political landscape of ancient Portugal, with tribal confederations and kingdoms vying for power and territory. These conflicts and alliances shaped the geopolitical dynamics of the region and set the stage for the later Roman conquest and integration of Lusitania.

Overall, the influence of the Iberian tribes and the Celts in ancient Portugal was instrumental in shaping the region's identity and laying the groundwork for its future development. Their cultural exchanges, technological innovations, and social interactions formed a rich tapestry of traditions that continues to resonate in modern Portuguese society.

The arrival and impact of the Phoenicians, Greeks, & Carthaginians
Chapter 1 of 'The History of Portugal' delves into the ancient roots of the region, exploring the significant influence of various civilizations on the land now known as Portugal. Among these early influencers were the Phoenicians, Greeks, and Carthaginians, whose arrival and impact played a crucial role in shaping the cultural, economic, and political landscape of ancient Portugal.

The Phoenicians, known for their seafaring prowess and extensive trade networks, first made their presence felt along the western coast of the Iberian Peninsula. They established trading posts and colonies, such as Gadir (modern-day Cádiz), which served as important hubs for commerce and cultural exchange. The Phoenicians introduced advanced maritime technology and navigational skills to the region, laying the foundation for future maritime endeavors by the Portuguese.

The Greeks also left their mark on ancient Portugal, particularly through their colonization efforts in regions like the Algarve. Greek settlements like Alcácer do Sal became centers of trade and cultural diffusion, where Greek artistic and architectural influences mingled with local traditions. The Greeks brought with them new agricultural techniques, artistic styles, and philosophical ideas that enriched the cultural fabric of ancient Portugal.

The Carthaginians, a powerful North African civilization with a formidable military and commercial empire, expanded their influence into the Iberian Peninsula, including present-day Portugal. Carthage's strategic interests in the region led to conflicts with local tribes and other Mediterranean powers, such as Rome. The Carthaginians established colonies and trading outposts along the coast, further connecting Portugal to the wider Mediterranean world.

The interactions between the Phoenicians, Greeks, and Carthaginians and the indigenous populations of ancient Portugal were complex and multifaceted. Trade flourished, bringing exotic goods, technology, and ideas to the region. Cultural exchanges led to the adoption of new customs, languages, and religious practices, enriching the diverse tapestry of ancient Portuguese society.

However, these interactions were not always peaceful, as competition for resources, territory, and influence sometimes led to conflicts and power struggles. The arrival of the Carthaginians, in particular, brought about military confrontations with other Mediterranean powers, most notably the Roman Republic, which ultimately led to the incorporation of the Iberian Peninsula into the Roman Empire.

In conclusion, the arrival and impact of the Phoenicians, Greeks, and Carthaginians in ancient Portugal marked a significant chapter in the region's history. Their contributions to trade, culture, and technology laid the groundwork for the later development of Portugal as a maritime power and a crossroads of global exchange. The legacy of these ancient civilizations continues to resonate in the cultural heritage and historical identity of modern-day Portugal.

Chapter 2

Roman Lusitania

Roman conquest and the integration of Lusitania into the Roman Empire

The Roman conquest of Lusitania marked a significant turning point in the history of Portugal, shaping its culture, infrastructure, and economy for centuries to come. The integration of Lusitania into the vast Roman Empire brought about profound changes that left a lasting impact on the region.

Roman conquest and assimilation were characterized by military campaigns led by Roman generals such as Decimus Junius Brutus and Julius Caesar. The Lusitanian tribes, known for their fierce resistance, were eventually subdued by the Romans through a combination of military might, diplomacy, and strategic alliances. The conquest resulted in the establishment of Roman rule over Lusitania, bringing the region under the governance of the Roman Republic and later the Roman Empire.

Under Roman rule, Lusitania experienced a period of significant development and transformation. Roman culture, architecture, and legal systems were introduced, leading to the Romanization of the local population. Roman cities, such as Emerita Augusta (modern-day Mérida), Pax Julia (modern-day Beja), and Olisipo (modern-day Lisbon), were founded or expanded, becoming centers of Roman administration, trade, and culture.

The Romans also invested heavily in infrastructure projects, constructing roads, bridges, aqueducts, and public buildings that facilitated communication and trade within the region. The network of Roman roads, such as the Via Lusitanorum, connected Lusitania to other parts of the empire, enabling the efficient movement of goods and people.

Economically, Lusitania thrived under Roman rule, benefiting from increased agricultural productivity, mining activities, and trade networks. The region's fertile lands were cultivated for the production of olive oil, wine, and grain, which were exported to other parts of the empire. Mining operations in areas rich in minerals, such as copper and silver, contributed to the region's prosperity and attracted Roman settlers and entrepreneurs.

The decline of Roman rule in Lusitania began in the 5th century AD with the incursions of Germanic tribes, such as the Visigoths, into the Iberian Peninsula. The Visigothic conquest of Lusitania marked the end of Roman control in the region and the beginning of a new chapter in its history.

Despite the eventual fall of the Western Roman Empire, the legacy of Roman Lusitania endured through the preservation of Roman infrastructure, language, and customs in Portugal. The integration of Lusitania into the Roman Empire not only shaped the physical landscape of the region but also influenced its cultural identity and historical development in the centuries that followed.

Roman culture, infrastructure, and economy in ancient Portugal
During the Roman period, Lusitania, which is now modern-day Portugal, experienced significant cultural, infrastructural, and economic developments under Roman rule. This chapter delves into the impact of Roman culture, infrastructure, and economy on ancient Portugal.

Roman Culture in Lusitania: The Romans brought their rich and sophisticated culture to Lusitania, influencing various aspects of life in the region. They introduced Latin as the official language, which eventually evolved into the Portuguese language spoken today. Roman architecture and engineering also left a lasting mark on the landscape of Lusitania, with the construction of roads, bridges, aqueducts, and impressive buildings such as temples, theaters, and amphitheaters.

Infrastructure: One of the most enduring legacies of Roman rule in Lusitania was the development of a well-organized and efficient infrastructure. The Romans constructed a network of roads that connected major cities and settlements, facilitating trade, communication, and military movements. The most famous of these roads was the Via Lusitania, which linked the region to the rest of the Roman Empire. Additionally, the Romans built aqueducts to supply water to urban centers and agricultural lands, enhancing the quality of life for the inhabitants of Lusitania.

Economy: The Roman presence in Lusitania also had a profound impact on the region's economy. The Romans introduced advanced agricultural techniques, such as irrigation and crop rotation, which led to increased productivity and prosperity. Lusitania became known for its production of olive oil, wine, and grain, which were exported to other parts of the Roman Empire. The region also benefited from mining activities, particularly the extraction of gold, silver, and other minerals.

Trade and Commerce: Under Roman rule, Lusitania became an important center of trade and commerce. The region's strategic location on the Atlantic coast allowed for easy access to maritime trade routes, leading to the growth of port cities such as Olisipo (modern-day Lisbon) and Portus Cale (modern-day Porto). These ports became bustling hubs of economic activity, facilitating the exchange of goods with other Roman provinces and beyond. The establishment of marketplaces and trade guilds further boosted the region's economy and stimulated cultural exchange.

Cultural Exchange: The Roman presence in Lusitania also facilitated cultural exchange and interaction with other parts of the Roman Empire. Romanization spread throughout the region, influencing local customs, beliefs, and traditions. The adoption of Roman religious practices, such as the worship of Roman gods and goddesses, and the construction of temples and shrines reflected this cultural assimilation. Roman influence also extended to the arts, literature, and entertainment, enriching the cultural landscape of Lusitania.

In conclusion, the Roman period in Lusitania was a time of significant transformation, characterized by the spread of Roman culture, the development of infrastructure, and the expansion of the region's economy. The legacy of Roman rule in ancient Portugal continues to be seen in the language, architecture, and economic activities of the region, shaping its historical identity and cultural heritage.

The Decline of Roman Rule and the Arrival of the Visigoths

After centuries of Roman domination, the Iberian Peninsula witnessed a period of significant change marked by the decline of Roman rule and the arrival of the Visigoths. This transitional period shaped the future of Portugal and set the stage for the emergence of new powers in the region.

The Roman conquest of Lusitania had brought stability, infrastructure, and a thriving economy to the region. However, by the 5th century AD, the Western Roman Empire was in decline, facing internal strife, economic challenges, and external threats. The once mighty empire was struggling to maintain control over its vast territories, including Lusitania.

In this backdrop of instability, the Visigoths, a Germanic tribe from Central Europe, seized the opportunity to expand their influence into the Iberian Peninsula. Led by their king Alaric, the Visigoths crossed the Pyrenees Mountains and launched a series of military campaigns to assert their dominance over the region.

The Visigothic invasion of Lusitania marked the beginning of a new era in Portuguese history. The Roman infrastructure and institutions began to crumble as the Visigoths established their rule over the territory. The Visigothic society was characterized by a warrior aristocracy, a complex legal system, and a fusion of Roman and Germanic cultural elements.

The arrival of the Visigoths brought about significant changes in the political, social, and economic landscape of ancient Portugal. The Roman administrative structures were gradually replaced by Visigothic governance, with local elites playing a key role in the new order. The Visigoths also introduced their own laws and customs, shaping the legal framework of the region for centuries to come.

The decline of Roman rule and the arrival of the Visigoths had a profound impact on the cultural identity of Portugal. The fusion of Roman, Visigothic, and later Islamic influences created a rich tapestry of traditions, languages, and beliefs that would shape the diverse heritage of the Portuguese people.

The Visigothic period in Portugal was characterized by a blend of continuity and change, as the new rulers sought to adapt to the complex realities of governing a diverse population. The legacy of the Visigoths would endure through the centuries, influencing the development of medieval Portugal and leaving a lasting imprint on the country's historical narrative.

In conclusion, the decline of Roman rule and the arrival of the Visigoths marked a pivotal moment in the history of Portugal. This period of transition laid the foundation for the emergence of new powers and cultural influences that would shape the destiny of the region for centuries to come. The Visigothic era represents a fascinating chapter in the rich tapestry of Portuguese history, highlighting the dynamic interactions between different peoples and civilizations in shaping the identity of the nation.

Chapter 3

The Islamic Period

The Moorish invasion and the establishment of Al-Andalus
The Moorish invasion and the establishment of Al-Andalus marked a significant period in the history of Portugal, shaping its culture, economy, and identity for centuries to come. This chapter delves into the impact of the Islamic conquest on the Iberian Peninsula, particularly in the region that would later become Portugal.

The Moorish invasion of the Iberian Peninsula in the early 8th century brought about a profound transformation in the political and cultural landscape of the region. Led by the Umayyad Caliphate, Muslim forces quickly conquered the Visigothic Kingdom of Hispania, which encompassed modern-day Portugal and Spain. The Moors, as the Muslim conquerors were known, established the Islamic state of Al-Andalus, with its capital in Cordoba, marking the beginning of a new era in Iberian history.

Under Moorish rule, Al-Andalus experienced a period of remarkable cultural and economic prosperity. The Moors introduced advanced irrigation techniques, agricultural practices, and architectural innovations that significantly influenced the development of the region. The cities of Al-Andalus, including Lisbon and Faro in present-day Portugal, became centers of learning, trade, and artistic expression, fostering a rich and diverse cultural environment.

The Islamic period in Portugal was characterized by a harmonious coexistence of Muslim, Christian, and Jewish communities, known for their intellectual and artistic contributions. Scholars, poets, and philosophers from different religious and cultural backgrounds collaborated and exchanged ideas, leading to a flourishing of knowledge and creativity.

The economy of Al-Andalus thrived on trade with North Africa and the Middle East, facilitated by its strategic location on the Mediterranean coast. Portuguese ports, such as Silves and Alcácer do Sal, became important hubs for commerce, connecting the region to broader networks of exchange and fostering economic growth.

Despite the cultural and economic achievements of Al-Andalus, the period was also marked by intermittent conflicts and power struggles among Muslim factions, as well as tensions with Christian kingdoms in the north. The Christian Reconquista, a long-term campaign to reclaim the Iberian Peninsula from Muslim rule, gained momentum during this time, laying the groundwork for the emergence of distinct Christian kingdoms, including the County of Portugal.

The Moorish invasion and the establishment of Al-Andalus left a lasting imprint on the history of Portugal, shaping its identity as a nation at the crossroads of different civilizations. The legacy of Islamic rule is evident in the architecture, language, and cultural practices of Portugal, reflecting the enduring influence of the Moors on the country's heritage.

Overall, the Moorish invasion and the establishment of Al-Andalus represent a pivotal chapter in the history of Portugal, highlighting the complex interactions between different religious and cultural groups and the enduring legacy of Islamic civilization on the Iberian Peninsula.

Cultural and economic developments under Islamic rule
During the Islamic Period in Portugal, which lasted from the 8th to the 12th centuries, the region experienced significant cultural and economic developments under Moorish rule. The Moorish invasion of the Iberian Peninsula in 711 AD led to the establishment of Al-Andalus, an Islamic territory that included parts of modern-day Portugal. This period had a lasting impact on Portuguese history, shaping its culture, architecture, agriculture, and economy.

Cultural Developments:
Under Islamic rule, Portugal experienced a flourishing of arts, science, and architecture. The Moors brought with them advanced knowledge in mathematics, astronomy, medicine, and philosophy, which greatly influenced the culture of the region. Islamic scholars translated Greek and Roman texts into Arabic, preserving and expanding upon ancient knowledge. This cultural exchange enriched Portuguese society and contributed to the development of a unique blend of Islamic, Christian, and Jewish traditions.

One of the most notable cultural achievements of the Islamic Period in Portugal was the construction of elaborate architectural monuments, such as mosques, palaces, and fortresses. The Moorish influence can be seen in the intricate geometric patterns, horseshoe arches, and decorative tilework that adorn many buildings in Portugal, particularly in the southern regions.

Islamic rule also had a profound impact on the language and literature of Portugal. Arabic became the language of administration, trade, and culture, leading to the incorporation of Arabic words into the Portuguese language. This linguistic influence can still be observed in modern Portuguese vocabulary.

Economic Developments:
The Islamic Period brought significant economic prosperity to Portugal through trade, agriculture, and industry. The Moors introduced advanced irrigation techniques, such as the construction of aqueducts and water channels, which improved agricultural productivity and enabled the cultivation of crops like citrus fruits, almonds, and rice. The development of agriculture and trade routes facilitated the growth of urban centers and the establishment of bustling markets and commercial hubs.

Portugal became an important trading hub in the Mediterranean, connecting Europe with the Islamic world and Africa. The ports of Lisbon, Porto, and Faro thrived as centers of commerce, facilitating the exchange of goods, ideas, and technologies. The Moors also introduced new crops and products to Portugal, including sugar cane, cotton, silk, and spices, which further enriched the economy.

The Islamic Period in Portugal was characterized by a vibrant economy fueled by trade, agriculture, and craftsmanship. The legacy of this period can be seen in the cultural and architectural heritage of Portugal, as well as in the linguistic and economic influences that continue to shape the country's identity.

The Christian Reconquista and the Emergence of Portuguese Identity

The Christian Reconquista marked a pivotal period in the history of Portugal, shaping the country's identity and laying the foundations for its future as an independent nation. The Reconquista refers to the long process of Christian kingdoms in the Iberian Peninsula gradually retaking territories from Muslim rule. In the case of Portugal, this struggle against Islamic domination played a crucial role in defining Portuguese national identity.

The Moorish invasion in the 8th century brought Islamic rule to the Iberian Peninsula, including present-day Portugal. The establishment of Al-Andalus by the Moors led to a period of significant cultural and economic development, but it also sparked resistance among the Christian kingdoms in the north, including the emerging County of Portugal.

As the Reconquista gained momentum in the 11th and 12th centuries, the Christian rulers in the region began to push southwards, reclaiming territories from the Moors. One of the key figures in this process was Afonso Henriques, who would later become the first King of Portugal. Afonso Henriques played a crucial role in the Battle of Ourique in 1139, where he defeated the Moors and asserted his authority over the County of Portugal.

The Treaty of Zamora in 1143 marked a significant turning point, as it secured the recognition of Portuguese independence from the Kingdom of León. This treaty not only solidified Portugal's status as a separate political entity but also laid the groundwork for the establishment of the Kingdom of Portugal with Afonso Henriques as its king.

The emergence of Portuguese identity during the Reconquista was influenced by a combination of factors. The Christian struggle against Islamic rule fostered a sense of unity and solidarity among the various Christian kingdoms in the region, including Portugal. The shared goal of pushing back the Moors and reclaiming lost territories helped to forge a common sense of purpose and identity among the Christian rulers and their subjects.

Furthermore, the Reconquista also played a role in shaping Portugal's cultural and religious identity. The Christian kingdoms in the Iberian Peninsula, including Portugal, were deeply influenced by their Catholic faith, which became a defining feature of Portuguese identity. The Reconquista not only symbolized the Christian struggle against Islamic domination but also reinforced the ties between the Portuguese people and the Catholic Church.

In conclusion, the Christian Reconquista was a transformative period in Portuguese history that not only led to the establishment of an independent Portuguese kingdom but also played a crucial role in shaping Portuguese identity. The struggle against Islamic rule, the leadership of figures like Afonso Henriques, and the cultural and religious influences of the Christian faith all contributed to the emergence of a distinct Portuguese national identity that continues to resonate to this day.

Chapter 4

The Birth of Portugal

The County of Portugal and the role of Count Henry

The County of Portugal played a crucial role in the early history of Portugal, laying the foundation for the emergence of an independent nation. At the heart of this pivotal period was Count Henry, a key figure in the establishment of Portuguese identity and independence.

Count Henry, also known as Henry of Burgundy, was a nobleman from the House of Burgundy who arrived in the Iberian Peninsula in the 11th century. He married Theresa, a Galician noblewoman, and through this union, he became the Count of Portugal. Count Henry was a skilled military leader and administrator, known for his strategic vision and determination to expand his influence in the region.

Under Count Henry's leadership, the County of Portugal began to assert its autonomy from the Kingdom of Leon, which had long held sway over the territory. Count Henry's efforts to consolidate power and establish a distinct political entity laid the groundwork for the future Kingdom of Portugal.

One of Count Henry's most significant contributions was the promotion of Christianization and the encouragement of settlement in the region. He supported the construction of churches and monasteries, attracting clergy and settlers to the area. This helped to strengthen the Christian presence in Portugal and foster a sense of unity among the population.

Count Henry also played a crucial role in defending the County of Portugal against external threats, particularly from the Moors who controlled much of the Iberian Peninsula at the time. He led military campaigns to repel Moorish incursions and expand the territory under his control. His victories in battle and strategic alliances with neighboring rulers further enhanced the County of Portugal's prestige and power.

One of the defining moments in Count Henry's career was his support for his son, Afonso Henriques, in his quest for independence from Leon. Afonso Henriques would go on to become the first King of Portugal, establishing the nation as a separate entity from its neighbors. Count Henry's guidance and mentorship were instrumental in shaping Afonso Henriques' leadership skills and instilling in him a sense of national pride and determination.

In conclusion, the County of Portugal and the role of Count Henry were instrumental in shaping the early history of Portugal. Count Henry's leadership, military prowess, and dedication to the Christian cause laid the groundwork for the emergence of an independent Portuguese nation. His legacy continues to be celebrated in Portugal's national history as a founding figure whose vision and determination paved the way for the country's future prosperity and identity.

Afonso Henriques and the Battle of Ourique

Afonso Henriques, also known as Afonso I, was a pivotal figure in the history of Portugal and played a crucial role in the establishment of the Portuguese nation. Born in 1109, Afonso was the son of Count Henry of Burgundy and Teresa of León, making him a descendant of both Portuguese and Galician nobility. His upbringing was marked by the turbulent political landscape of the Iberian Peninsula, with conflicts between Christian and Muslim forces shaping his early years.

One of the defining moments in Afonso's life was the Battle of Ourique, which took place in 1139. This battle is considered a turning point in the history of Portugal as it marks the emergence of Afonso as a powerful leader and the beginning of the Portuguese independence movement. The circumstances leading up to the battle were complex, with Afonso facing internal opposition from his mother and external threats from both Muslim and Christian forces.

The Battle of Ourique was fought between the forces of Afonso and the Almoravid dynasty, a powerful Muslim empire that controlled much of the Iberian Peninsula at the time. Despite being outnumbered, Afonso displayed remarkable military skill and strategic acumen, leading his troops to a decisive victory over the Almoravid forces. The battle not only secured Afonso's position as a ruler but also boosted the morale of the Portuguese people and solidified the sense of national identity.

Following his victory at Ourique, Afonso declared himself King of Portugal, a title that was later confirmed by the Treaty of Zamora in 1143. This marked the official recognition of Portuguese independence from the Kingdom of León and laid the foundation for the future growth and expansion of the Portuguese kingdom. Afonso's reign as the first King of Portugal was marked by territorial conquests, administrative reforms, and diplomatic maneuvering to secure his kingdom's position in the region.

The Battle of Ourique and Afonso's subsequent coronation as King of Portugal were significant milestones in the history of the country, symbolizing the beginning of a new era of independence and self-determination. Afonso's legacy as a visionary leader and a skilled military commander continues to be celebrated in Portuguese history and culture, with numerous monuments and commemorations honoring his contributions to the nation.

In conclusion, Afonso Henriques and the Battle of Ourique are central to understanding the origins of Portugal as a nation and the enduring spirit of independence and resilience that has characterized the Portuguese people throughout history. Afonso's leadership and determination in the face of adversity have left a lasting legacy that continues to inspire generations of Portuguese citizens to this day.

Treaty of Zamora & the recognition of Portuguese independence
The Treaty of Zamora, signed in 1143, was a pivotal moment in Portuguese history that solidified the recognition of Portugal as an independent kingdom. This treaty marked the end of centuries of struggles for autonomy and laid the foundation for the establishment of a sovereign Portuguese state.

The context leading up to the Treaty of Zamora can be traced back to the County of Portugal, a territory in the northwest of the Iberian Peninsula ruled by the nobleman Count Henry. Count Henry, along with his son Afonso Henriques, played a crucial role in the fight for independence from the Kingdom of León. The Battle of Ourique in 1139, where Afonso Henriques emerged victorious, marked a turning point in the struggle for autonomy.

Following this decisive battle, negotiations between Afonso Henriques and King Alfonso VII of León led to the signing of the Treaty of Zamora in 1143. The treaty recognized Afonso Henriques as the legitimate ruler of Portugal and granted the new kingdom its independence from León. This formal acknowledgment of Portuguese sovereignty by a neighboring kingdom was a significant step towards establishing Portugal as a distinct political entity in the region.

The Treaty of Zamora not only secured Portugal's independence but also laid the groundwork for diplomatic relations with other European powers. The treaty set the stage for Portugal to forge alliances and establish itself as a player in the geopolitics of medieval Europe. It also paved the way for future territorial expansions and the consolidation of the Portuguese kingdom under Afonso Henriques and his successors.

The recognition of Portuguese independence through the Treaty of Zamora had far-reaching implications for the cultural, economic, and social development of the nascent kingdom. With a newfound sense of national identity and autonomy, Portugal was able to chart its own course and pursue its interests on the international stage. This newfound independence also allowed

Portugal to focus on internal governance, economic growth, and the expansion of its territories.

The Treaty of Zamora is a testament to the resilience and determination of the Portuguese people to secure their freedom and establish a sovereign nation. It symbolizes the beginning of a new chapter in Portuguese history, one marked by independence, self-determination, and a sense of national pride. The legacy of the Treaty of Zamora continues to resonate in modern Portugal, serving as a reminder of the country's long and storied journey towards nationhood.

Chapter 5

The Age of Expansion

The consolidation of the Portuguese kingdom

The consolidation of the Portuguese kingdom marked a crucial period in the history of Portugal, laying the foundation for the country's future as a major European power. This phase, which unfolded during the Age of Expansion, encompassed various political, military, and economic developments that solidified Portugal's territorial integrity and strengthened its position on the world stage.

During this time, Portugal faced internal and external challenges as it sought to unify its territories and assert its independence from neighboring kingdoms. One key figure in this process was Afonso Henriques, who played a pivotal role in establishing the County of Portugal and eventually securing recognition of Portuguese independence through the Treaty of Zamora.

Under Afonso Henriques' leadership, Portugal embarked on a series of military campaigns to expand its borders and consolidate its control over various regions. The Battle of Ourique, where Afonso Henriques allegedly received a divine vision that inspired his troops to victory, became a symbolic moment in Portuguese history, reinforcing the kingdom's sense of destiny and purpose.

The territorial expansion and consolidation of the Portuguese kingdom were further advanced through diplomatic alliances, strategic marriages, and the establishment of administrative structures. The role of Count Henry, Afonso Henriques' father, in laying the groundwork for the county's development cannot be understated, as his efforts set the stage for his son's successful reign.

The maritime discoveries and explorations that characterized the Age of Expansion also played a significant role in consolidating the Portuguese kingdom. Prince Henry the Navigator's vision and support for naval expeditions paved the way for Portuguese sailors like Vasco da Gama and Bartolomeu Dias to chart new territories and establish trading posts in Africa, Asia, and the Americas.

The economic prosperity resulting from these maritime ventures contributed to the kingdom's consolidation by enriching its coffers and expanding its influence in global trade networks. The establishment of the Portuguese Empire in key regions such as Brazil, India, and Macau further solidified Portugal's status as a major player in the Age of Discovery.

Culturally and intellectually, the consolidation of the Portuguese kingdom during this period saw the flourishing of arts, literature, and science. The exchange of ideas and knowledge with other civilizations, especially during the Islamic Period, enriched Portuguese society and contributed to its intellectual advancement.

Overall, the consolidation of the Portuguese kingdom was a multifaceted process that involved military conquests, diplomatic maneuvering, economic expansion, and cultural flourishing. This period laid the groundwork for Portugal's emergence as a global power and set the stage for its subsequent achievements and challenges in the centuries to come.

Maritime Discoveries & the Role of Prince Henry the Navigator
During the 15th century, Portugal experienced a period of great maritime exploration and discovery that would forever alter the course of world history. Central to this era of exploration was Prince Henry the Navigator, a member of the Portuguese royal family who played a pivotal role in promoting and supporting Portugal's maritime endeavors.

Prince Henry, also known as Infante Dom Henrique, was born in 1394 and was a passionate advocate for exploration and discovery. He established a navigational school in the town of Sagres, located in the southwestern tip of Portugal, where he gathered scholars, cartographers, sailors, and navigators to study the art of navigation and explore new trade routes.

One of Prince Henry's primary goals was to find a sea route to Asia in order to bypass the overland trade routes controlled by the Venetians and the Ottomans. He believed that by sailing around Africa, Portuguese explorers could reach the lucrative markets of the East Indies and establish direct trade links with Asian civilizations.

Under Prince Henry's patronage, Portuguese sailors embarked on a series of daring voyages along the coast of Africa, gradually pushing further southward in search of a sea route to Asia. One of the key achievements of these expeditions was the discovery of the Cape of Good Hope by Bartolomeu Dias in 1488, which proved that it was possible to sail around the southern tip of Africa.

Prince Henry's support for exploration also led to the discovery of new territories in the Atlantic Ocean. In 1419, Portuguese explorers discovered the island of Madeira, followed by the Azores in 1432 and Cape Verde in 1444. These discoveries not only expanded Portugal's territorial holdings but also laid the groundwork for further exploration and colonization in the Atlantic.

The maritime discoveries made during Prince Henry's lifetime laid the foundation for Portugal's future as a global maritime power. His visionary leadership and unwavering commitment to exploration paved the way for future Portuguese explorers, such as Vasco da Gama and Pedro Álvares Cabral, to achieve even greater feats of exploration and discovery.

Overall, Prince Henry the Navigator's role in promoting maritime exploration was instrumental in shaping Portugal's identity as a seafaring nation and in establishing its reputation as a pioneer in the Age of Discovery. His legacy continues to be celebrated as a symbol of Portugal's spirit of adventure and exploration, and his contributions have left an indelible mark on world history.

The voyages of Vasco da Gama, Bartolomeu Dias, and other explorers
The voyages of Vasco da Gama, Bartolomeu Dias, and other explorers marked a pivotal period in Portuguese history and the Age of Exploration. These intrepid explorers played a crucial role in expanding Portugal's influence and establishing the Portuguese Empire in Africa, Asia, and the Americas. Their voyages not only opened up new trade routes and opportunities but also contributed to the spread of European culture and technology across the globe.

Vasco da Gama is perhaps one of the most famous Portuguese explorers, known for his groundbreaking voyage to India. In 1497, da Gama set sail from Lisbon with the goal of reaching India by sea, bypassing the overland trade routes controlled by Arab and Venetian merchants. After a perilous journey around the Cape of Good Hope, da Gama successfully reached Calicut in India in 1498. This achievement not only established a direct sea route to India but also laid the foundation for Portuguese dominance in the Indian Ocean trade.

Bartolomeu Dias, another notable explorer, was the first European to sail around the southern tip of Africa, known as the Cape of Good Hope. In 1488, Dias embarked on his historic voyage commissioned by King John II of Portugal to explore the possibility of reaching India by sea. Dias successfully navigated the treacherous waters of the Cape, proving that a sea route to the East was feasible. His discovery paved the way for future explorers like da Gama to reach India and establish lucrative trade networks.

Other Portuguese explorers, such as Pedro Álvares Cabral, who is credited with the discovery of Brazil in 1500, and Ferdinand Magellan, who led the first expedition to circumnavigate the globe in 1519-1522, further expanded Portugal's global reach and influence. These explorers ventured into unknown territories, mapping new lands, establishing trade connections, and spreading European influence to distant corners of the world.

The voyages of these explorers not only brought wealth and prestige to Portugal but also had far-reaching consequences for world history. The establishment of trade routes to Asia and the Americas led to the exchange of goods, ideas, and cultures between continents, shaping the course of global trade and exploration for centuries to come. The Portuguese Empire's expansion into Africa, Asia, and the Americas set the stage for the Age of Discovery and the subsequent era of European colonialism.

In conclusion, the voyages of Vasco da Gama, Bartolomeu Dias, and other Portuguese explorers were instrumental in shaping the course of world history and establishing Portugal as a major player in the Age of Exploration. Their daring expeditions opened up new frontiers, expanded trade networks, and paved the way for the spread of European influence across the globe. The legacy of these explorers continues to be celebrated as a testament to human curiosity, courage, and the spirit of discovery that propelled the world into a new era of exploration and adventure.

The establishment of the Portuguese Empire in Africa, Asia, and the Americas
The establishment of the Portuguese Empire in Africa, Asia, and the Americas marked a significant chapter in world history, showcasing Portugal's prowess as a maritime power and its ambition to explore and conquer new territories. This period, known as the Age of Exploration or the Age of Discovery, was characterized by bold voyages of discovery, strategic alliances, and the establishment of trade routes that would shape global trade and politics for centuries to come.

Portugal's exploration and expansion into Africa began with the pioneering efforts of Prince Henry the Navigator, who sponsored expeditions along the West African coast in the 15th century. These explorations led to the discovery of new trade opportunities, including lucrative gold and ivory trade, as well as the establishment of trading posts and forts along the coast to facilitate trade and maintain Portuguese influence.

In Asia, Portuguese explorers like Vasco da Gama and Bartolomeu Dias played pivotal roles in opening up sea routes to the lucrative markets of the Indian Ocean. Da Gama's historic voyage around the Cape of Good Hope to India in 1498 not only established a direct sea route to Asia but also paved the way for the establishment of Portuguese trading posts and colonies in key locations such as Goa, Malacca, and Macau. The Portuguese Empire in Asia thrived on the spice trade, with spices like pepper, cinnamon, and nutmeg becoming highly sought-after commodities in Europe.

The Americas also played a crucial role in the expansion of the Portuguese Empire, with the discovery of Brazil in 1500 by Pedro Álvares Cabral. The colonization of Brazil marked the beginning of Portuguese presence in the New World, leading to the establishment of sugar plantations and the exploitation of indigenous labor. The Portuguese Empire in the Americas grew rapidly, with Brazil becoming a major source of wealth through the production of sugar, gold, and other valuable resources.

The establishment of the Portuguese Empire in Africa, Asia, and the Americas had profound economic, cultural, and political implications. The empire's control over key trade routes and resources brought immense wealth and power to Portugal, enabling the country to assert its influence on the global stage. The exchange of goods, ideas, and technologies between Europe, Africa, Asia, and the Americas during this period also laid the foundation for a more interconnected and globalized world.

However, the expansion of the Portuguese Empire was not without its challenges. Competition from other European powers, conflicts with local populations, and the hardships of navigating unknown waters and territories posed significant obstacles to Portugal's imperial ambitions. Moreover, the legacy of colonization and exploitation left a complex and lasting impact on the regions under Portuguese control, shaping their social, cultural, and political landscapes for generations to come.

In conclusion, the establishment of the Portuguese Empire in Africa, Asia, and the Americas was a defining chapter in Portugal's history, showcasing the country's spirit of exploration, enterprise, and ambition. This period of discovery and conquest not only expanded Portugal's influence and wealth but also contributed to the shaping of a more interconnected and diverse world. The legacy of the Portuguese Empire continues to resonate in the cultures, economies, and societies of the regions it once ruled, underscoring the enduring impact of Portugal's imperial past on the modern world.

Chapter 6

The Golden Age of Portugal

The height of Portuguese power and wealth

During the Golden Age of Portugal, the country experienced a period of unprecedented power and wealth that solidified its position as a major player in global affairs. This era, which spanned from the 15th to the 16th centuries, was characterized by a series of maritime discoveries, colonial expansion, and cultural achievements that reshaped the course of history.

One of the key factors that contributed to the height of Portuguese power and wealth was the pioneering spirit of its explorers and navigators. Led by Prince Henry the Navigator, Portuguese sailors embarked on daring voyages of discovery that expanded the known world and opened up new trade routes. Explorers such as Vasco da Gama, Bartolomeu Dias, and Ferdinand Magellan ventured into uncharted waters, braving treacherous seas and unknown dangers to reach distant lands in Africa, Asia, and the Americas. These expeditions not only brought back valuable resources such as spices, gold, and exotic goods but also established Portugal as a major player in global trade and commerce.

The establishment of the Portuguese Empire in Africa, Asia, and the Americas was another defining feature of this period. Through a series of strategic alliances, military conquests, and trading posts, Portugal carved out a vast overseas empire that stretched from Brazil to India to Macau. Portuguese colonies became centers of trade, culture, and power, enriching the motherland with wealth and resources while spreading Portuguese influence and language across the globe.

The wealth generated from overseas trade and colonial enterprises fueled a period of cultural and scientific achievement known as the Portuguese Renaissance. The influx of riches from the spice trade and other ventures enabled Portuguese monarchs, nobles, and merchants to patronize the arts, literature, and architecture, leading to a flourishing of creativity and innovation. Portuguese artists such as Vasco Fernandes, Gregório Lopes, and Nuno Gonçalves produced masterpieces that reflected the cosmopolitan nature of Portugal's empire, blending European, African, and Asian influences into a unique cultural synthesis.

The impact of the spice trade and colonial enterprises on Portugal's economy cannot be overstated. The influx of gold, silver, and other precious metals from overseas enriched the country's coffers and transformed it into a major economic power in Europe. The establishment of trading posts, plantations, and slave markets in Africa, Asia, and the Americas created a lucrative network of commerce that brought immense profits to Portuguese traders and merchants. The wealth generated from these ventures funded ambitious public works projects, such as the construction of palaces, churches, and fortresses, that showcased Portugal's newfound prosperity and power.

In conclusion, the height of Portuguese power and wealth during the Golden Age was a transformative period in the country's history that left a lasting legacy on the world. Through a combination of maritime exploration, colonial expansion, and cultural achievement, Portugal rose to prominence as a global superpower that shaped the course of history and left an indelible mark on the world.

Cultural and scientific achievements during the Age of Discovery

During the Age of Discovery, Portugal experienced a cultural and scientific renaissance that played a significant role in shaping the course of world history. This period, spanning from the 15th to the 17th centuries, was marked by a flourishing of intellectual and artistic endeavors that propelled Portugal to the forefront of European civilization.

One of the most notable cultural achievements of this era was the blending of diverse influences from around the world. Portuguese explorers, traders, and missionaries established contact with different cultures across Africa, Asia, and the Americas, leading to a rich exchange of ideas, knowledge, and technologies. This cultural interaction gave rise to a vibrant cosmopolitan society in Portugal, where diverse traditions, languages, and artistic styles coexisted and influenced each other.

In the realm of science, the Age of Discovery saw remarkable advancements in navigation, cartography, and astronomy. Portuguese sailors pioneered new maritime techniques and navigational instruments that revolutionized sea travel and exploration. The founding of navigation schools in Portugal, such as the famous School of Sagres established by Prince Henry the Navigator, provided a solid educational foundation for future generations of explorers and seafarers.

Cartography also flourished during this period, with Portuguese mapmakers creating detailed and accurate charts of previously uncharted territories. The famous navigational charts known as portolanos became essential tools for sailors, guiding them safely through unknown waters and enabling the expansion of Portuguese maritime trade and colonization.

In the field of astronomy, Portuguese scientists made significant contributions to the study of celestial navigation and the mapping of the stars. The astronomical observations conducted by Portuguese explorers during their voyages not only improved navigation techniques but also contributed to the broader scientific understanding of the universe.

The cultural and scientific achievements of the Age of Discovery were not limited to the realm of exploration and navigation. Portuguese scholars and artists also made important contributions to literature, art, and music during this period. The flourishing of the Portuguese Renaissance, with its emphasis on humanism, creativity, and intellectual curiosity, produced a wealth of literary works, paintings, and music that reflected the spirit of exploration and discovery that characterized the age.

Overall, the cultural and scientific achievements of the Age of Discovery in Portugal were a testament to the country's spirit of innovation, curiosity, and openness to the world. This period of exploration and exchange laid the foundation for Portugal's emergence as a global power and left a lasting legacy that continues to inspire and influence contemporary culture and science.

The impact of the spice trade and colonial enterprises
The impact of the spice trade and colonial enterprises on Portugal played a crucial role in shaping the country's history and

global influence during the Age of Exploration. This period marked a significant shift in world trade and power dynamics, with Portugal emerging as a key player in the race for spices and colonial dominance.

The spice trade was a lucrative and highly sought-after industry due to the high demand for exotic spices such as pepper, cinnamon, cloves, and nutmeg in Europe. These spices were not only prized for their culinary uses but also for their medicinal and preservative properties. The control of the spice trade routes was therefore a strategic priority for European powers looking to gain wealth and influence in the global market.

Portugal's geographical location on the western coast of the Iberian Peninsula gave it a strategic advantage in exploring new trade routes to Asia. Portuguese explorers such as Vasco da Gama and Bartolomeu Dias played a pivotal role in navigating the treacherous waters around the Cape of Good Hope and establishing direct sea routes to the spice-rich lands of India and the East Indies.

The establishment of these maritime trade routes not only brought a steady supply of valuable spices to Europe but also opened up new opportunities for Portuguese colonial expansion. Portugal's early overseas empire included territories in Africa, Asia, and the Americas, where they set up trading posts, forts, and colonies to facilitate the trade of spices, gold, slaves, and other commodities.

The colonial enterprises of Portugal had far-reaching economic, political, and cultural impacts on both the colonizers and the colonized regions. In terms of economics, the influx of spices and other exotic goods from overseas bolstered Portugal's economy and fueled the growth of trade and commerce. The Portuguese Empire became a major player in the global economy, connecting distant lands and facilitating the exchange of goods, ideas, and technologies.

Politically, the control of overseas territories allowed Portugal to expand its influence and power on the world stage. The establishment of colonies provided a source of wealth and resources for the crown, as well as strategic military outposts to protect Portuguese interests in the region. However, this expansion also led to conflicts with other European powers competing for control of overseas territories, leading to rivalries and power struggles that shaped the course of world history.

Culturally, the interactions between the Portuguese and the indigenous populations in the colonies resulted in the exchange of languages, religions, and traditions. The blending of European and local cultures gave rise to unique societies with diverse identities, shaping the cultural landscape of both the colonizers and the colonized.

In conclusion, the impact of the spice trade and colonial enterprises on Portugal was profound and far-reaching, shaping the country's history, economy, and global influence. The Age of Exploration marked a pivotal moment in world history, where Portugal's quest for spices and colonial dominance left a lasting legacy that continues to influence the nation and its relationships with the rest of the world.

Chapter 7

The Iberian Union and the Restoration

The dynastic crisis and the union with Spain
The dynastic crisis and the union with Spain marked a tumultuous period in Portuguese history, characterized by political intrigue, power struggles, and the loss of independence. This chapter delves into the events that led to the union of Portugal with Spain and the subsequent struggle for restoration.

Background of the Dynastic Crisis:
The dynastic crisis in Portugal was triggered by the death of King Sebastian in 1578 without leaving an heir. This event plunged the country into a succession crisis, as several claimants vied for the throne. The leading contenders were King Philip II of Spain, who was also a nephew of King Sebastian, and Dom António, Prior of Crato, a distant relative of the royal family.

The Union with Spain:
In 1580, after a brief period of political chaos and uncertainty, the Cortes (parliament) of Portugal recognized Philip II of Spain as the legitimate heir to the Portuguese throne. This decision effectively led to the union of the crowns of Spain and Portugal, as Philip II became the first king of the Iberian Union.

Impact on Portugal:
The union with Spain had significant implications for Portugal. While it brought a period of political stability and economic prosperity under the Spanish Habsburg monarchy, it also led to a

loss of autonomy and independence for the Portuguese kingdom. Portuguese institutions were gradually assimilated into the Spanish administration, and Portuguese nobility found themselves marginalized in favor of Spanish interests.

Resistance and the Restoration:
Despite initial support for the union with Spain, discontent began to simmer among the Portuguese population. The imposition of Spanish policies, heavy taxation, and cultural assimilation efforts fueled resentment and resistance against Spanish rule. This discontent eventually culminated in the Portuguese Restoration War, which began in 1640 with the successful rebellion against Spanish rule.

The Braganza Dynasty:
The Portuguese Restoration War led to the end of Spanish dominion over Portugal and the establishment of the Braganza dynasty. Dom João IV, Duke of Braganza, was proclaimed king in 1640, marking the restoration of Portuguese independence and sovereignty. The Braganza dynasty would go on to rule Portugal for over two centuries and play a pivotal role in shaping the nation's future.

Legacy of the Union and Restoration:
The Iberian Union and the subsequent Restoration period left a lasting impact on Portuguese history and identity. The experience of foreign domination and the struggle for independence reinforced a sense of national pride and resilience among the Portuguese people. The events of this period also underscored the importance of defending Portugal's sovereignty and cultural heritage against external threats.

In conclusion, the dynastic crisis and union with Spain represented a challenging chapter in Portugal's history, marked by political upheaval, foreign intervention, and ultimately, the triumph of national identity and independence. The legacy of this period continues to resonate in Portugal's collective memory and serves as a reminder of the enduring spirit of resilience and perseverance that defines the Portuguese nation.

The Portuguese Restoration War and the end of Spanish rule
The dynastic crisis and the union with Spain, The Portuguese Restoration War and the end of Spanish rule, The reign of the Braganza dynasty and the rebuilding of the nation

The Portuguese Restoration War was a significant conflict that took place between 1640 and 1668, marking the end of Spanish rule over Portugal and the restoration of Portuguese independence. The war was the culmination of years of discontent and resistance against Spanish domination, which had been imposed following the dynastic crisis that led to the Iberian Union in 1580.

The roots of the Portuguese Restoration War can be traced back to the death of King Sebastian of Portugal in 1578, which triggered a succession crisis. With no direct heir to the throne, several claimants vied for power, leading to a power vacuum that was exploited by King Philip II of Spain, who also had a claim to the Portuguese throne. Philip II invaded Portugal in 1580, defeated the Portuguese forces, and established Spanish control over the country, creating the Iberian Union.

Under Spanish rule, Portugal experienced economic exploitation, political repression, and cultural assimilation, leading to widespread discontent among the Portuguese population. The Portuguese nobility and clergy, in particular, resented Spanish interference in Portuguese affairs and the erosion of their privileges and autonomy.

The turning point came in 1640 when a group of conspirators led by the Duke of Braganza orchestrated a successful coup against Spanish rule. On December 1, 1640, the conspirators proclaimed John IV of Braganza as King of Portugal, initiating the Portuguese Restoration War. The Portuguese forces, supported by popular uprisings and foreign allies such as France and England, engaged in a protracted struggle against the Spanish armies.

The war was characterized by a series of military campaigns, sieges, and battles, as both sides fought for control of strategic territories and cities. The Portuguese forces, led by skilled commanders such as Dom António Luís de Meneses and Dom João de Mascarenhas, displayed resilience and determination in the face of superior Spanish forces.

One of the key turning points in the war was the Battle of Montijo in 1644, where the Portuguese army achieved a decisive victory over the Spanish forces, boosting morale and weakening Spanish control over Portugal. Over the following years, the Portuguese forces continued to make significant gains, gradually pushing the Spanish armies out of Portuguese territory.

The war finally came to an end in 1668 with the signing of the Treaty of Lisbon, which recognized Portuguese independence and the restoration of the Braganza dynasty to the Portuguese throne. The war marked the end of over six decades of Spanish rule and the beginning of a new era of Portuguese sovereignty and independence.

The Portuguese Restoration War had profound implications for Portugal's national identity and future development. It reaffirmed Portugal's distinct cultural and historical heritage, strengthened the monarchy under the Braganza dynasty, and laid the foundations for a period of political stability and economic growth. The war also highlighted the resilience and determination of the Portuguese people in the face of foreign domination, shaping Portugal's sense of national pride and independence for centuries to come.

Reign of the Braganza dynasty & the rebuilding of the nation
The reign of the Braganza dynasty marked a significant period in the history of Portugal, characterized by the nation's struggle for independence and rebuilding after the tumultuous period of the Iberian Union. The Braganza dynasty, established in the 17th century, played a crucial role in shaping the political landscape and national identity of Portugal.

The Braganza dynasty came to power following the Portuguese Restoration War, a conflict that erupted as a result of the dynastic crisis and the union with Spain under the Habsburg monarchy. The war, led by John IV of Portugal, culminated in the recognition of Portuguese independence with the signing of the Treaty of Lisbon in 1668. This marked the beginning of the

Braganza dynasty's rule and the rebuilding of the nation after years of foreign domination.

Under the Braganza rulers, particularly during the reign of John IV and his successors, Portugal witnessed a period of stability and consolidation of power. The dynasty focused on strengthening the country's institutions, economy, and military capabilities to secure its independence and protect its borders. They also sought to enhance Portugal's international standing and restore its influence in global affairs.

One of the key achievements of the Braganza dynasty was the establishment of diplomatic alliances with other European powers, particularly England. These alliances were crucial in safeguarding Portugal's interests and ensuring its security in a volatile geopolitical environment. The diplomatic efforts of the Braganza rulers helped to secure Portugal's place among the European powers and protect its territorial integrity.

In addition to diplomatic initiatives, the Braganza dynasty also made significant contributions to the cultural and artistic development of Portugal. The reign of King John V, in particular, is known as the "Golden Age" of Portuguese art and culture. The king's patronage of the arts led to the construction of magnificent palaces, churches, and monuments that still stand as testaments to Portugal's rich cultural heritage.

Furthermore, the Braganza dynasty played a crucial role in promoting religious tolerance and fostering a climate of intellectual and artistic flourishing. The period saw the rise of Portuguese literature, music, and architecture, with many renowned artists and scholars making significant contributions to the cultural legacy of the nation.

Overall, the reign of the Braganza dynasty was a transformative period in Portuguese history, characterized by efforts to rebuild the nation, assert its independence, and promote cultural and intellectual achievements. The dynasty's legacy continues to be felt in modern Portugal, as the country draws inspiration from its rich historical heritage and strives to uphold the values of independence, diplomacy, and cultural excellence established during the Braganza era.

Chapter 8

The Enlightenment and Reform

The Pombaline reforms and modernization efforts under the Marquis of Pombal

The Pombaline reforms, also known as the Marquis of Pombal reforms, were a series of significant changes implemented in Portugal during the 18th century under the leadership of Sebastião José de Carvalho e Melo, the Marquis of Pombal. These reforms were aimed at modernizing and restructuring various aspects of Portuguese society, economy, and governance in order to strengthen the nation and enhance its position in Europe. The period of Pombal's reforms, which lasted from 1750 to 1777, marked a pivotal moment in Portuguese history and had a lasting impact on the country's development.

One of the key areas of focus for the Pombaline reforms was economic modernization. Pombal implemented policies to promote industrial development, encourage trade, and boost agricultural productivity. He sought to reduce Portugal's economic dependence on foreign powers and enhance the nation's self-sufficiency. Pombal also established state-sponsored manufacturing enterprises and promoted the growth of industries such as textiles, ceramics, and wine production. These efforts aimed to stimulate economic growth and create new sources of revenue for the Portuguese government.

In addition to economic reforms, Pombal also undertook significant changes in the administrative and judicial systems of

Portugal. He reorganized the bureaucracy, centralizing power in the hands of the monarch and reducing the influence of the nobility and clergy. Pombal implemented measures to improve the efficiency and transparency of government institutions, including the establishment of new regulatory bodies and the implementation of stricter laws and regulations. These reforms aimed to streamline government operations, reduce corruption, and increase accountability in public administration.

Furthermore, the Pombaline reforms included initiatives to modernize education and promote scientific and cultural development in Portugal. Pombal established new schools and educational institutions, emphasizing the importance of science, technology, and intellectual progress. He also supported the arts and literature, encouraging the production of works that celebrated Portuguese culture and history. Pombal's efforts to promote education and cultural development laid the foundation for a more enlightened and progressive society in Portugal.

The Pombaline reforms were not without controversy, as they faced resistance from traditionalist factions within Portuguese society. Critics of Pombal accused him of authoritarianism and centralization of power, and his reforms were met with opposition from conservative groups. Despite these challenges, Pombal persisted in his efforts to modernize Portugal and strengthen the nation's position in Europe.

Overall, the Pombaline reforms were a transformative period in Portuguese history, marking a shift towards modernization and progress. The legacy of these reforms can be seen in the economic, political, and cultural developments that shaped Portugal in the following centuries. Sebastião José de Carvalho e

Melo, the Marquis of Pombal, is remembered as a key figure in Portugal's history, whose reforms laid the groundwork for the nation's future growth and prosperity.

The impact of the Napoleonic Wars and the Peninsular War
The impact of the Napoleonic Wars and the Peninsular War on Portugal was profound and far-reaching, shaping the nation's history and identity in significant ways. The Napoleonic Wars, which were a series of conflicts fought between France and various European powers between 1803 and 1815, had a direct impact on Portugal due to its strategic location on the Iberian Peninsula. The Peninsular War, which was a part of the Napoleonic Wars, specifically focused on the Iberian Peninsula and involved the French invasion of Spain and Portugal.

One of the key impacts of the Napoleonic Wars and the Peninsular War on Portugal was the invasion and occupation of the country by French forces under Napoleon Bonaparte. In 1807, French troops under General Junot invaded Portugal, leading to the royal family fleeing to Brazil to escape capture. This event marked the beginning of a period of turmoil and resistance in Portugal, as the Portuguese people rallied against the French occupation and fought to maintain their independence.

The Peninsular War also had a significant impact on Portugal's economy and society. The war disrupted trade and commerce, leading to economic hardship and social unrest. The Portuguese population suffered from food shortages, inflation, and increased taxation imposed by the French occupiers, further exacerbating the challenges faced by the country during this period.

Despite the challenges posed by the French occupation, the Peninsular War also provided an opportunity for Portugal to strengthen its ties with its traditional ally, Great Britain. The British played a crucial role in supporting the Portuguese resistance against the French, providing military assistance and naval support to help drive the French forces out of the country. The alliances formed during the Peninsular War would have lasting implications for Portugal's foreign relations and strategic interests in the years to come.

Furthermore, the Napoleonic Wars and the Peninsular War had a lasting impact on Portugal's political landscape. The war fueled nationalist sentiments and a sense of unity among the Portuguese people, leading to a resurgence of patriotism and a desire for greater autonomy and independence. The events of the war also contributed to the decline of the Portuguese monarchy and paved the way for political reforms and changes in governance that would shape the country's future trajectory.

In conclusion, the Napoleonic Wars and the Peninsular War had a complex and multifaceted impact on Portugal, influencing its economy, society, politics, and national identity. The war tested the resilience and determination of the Portuguese people, fostering a spirit of resistance and unity that would define Portugal's path towards modernization and independence. The lessons learned from this turbulent period in Portuguese history continue to resonate today, reminding us of the enduring legacy of struggle and perseverance in the face of adversity.

The transfer of the royal court to Brazil and the independence of Brazil

The transfer of the royal court to Brazil and the independence of Brazil marked a significant turning point in Portuguese and Brazilian history, with far-reaching consequences for both nations. This event was precipitated by the Napoleonic invasion of Portugal in 1807, which forced the Portuguese royal family to flee to Brazil for safety and to establish Rio de Janeiro as the new capital of the Portuguese Empire.

The transfer of the royal court to Brazil had profound political, economic, and social implications for both Portugal and Brazil. In the context of Portugal, the presence of the royal family in Brazil led to a power vacuum in the homeland, which allowed for political turmoil and the emergence of conflicting factions vying for control. This period of instability ultimately laid the groundwork for the liberal movements that would lead to the establishment of a constitutional monarchy in Portugal in the 19th century.

Meanwhile, in Brazil, the presence of the royal court catalyzed significant cultural and economic developments. The influx of Portuguese aristocracy and intellectuals to Brazil brought with them new ideas and cultural influences that contributed to the flourishing of arts, literature, and education in the colony. Additionally, the opening of Brazilian ports to international trade under the royal decree of 1808 led to increased economic activity and the expansion of Brazil's role as a key player in the Atlantic trade network.

The transfer of the royal court also played a crucial role in paving the way for Brazil's eventual independence from Portugal. The

59

royal family's extended stay in Brazil and their establishment of a separate administrative and political center in Rio de Janeiro fostered a sense of Brazilian identity and autonomy. This, coupled with growing discontent among the Brazilian elite with Portuguese colonial rule and the desire for greater political representation, set the stage for the movement towards independence.

The independence of Brazil was formally declared on September 7, 1822, with the proclamation of Prince Pedro as Emperor Pedro I of Brazil. This marked the culmination of a process that had been brewing for years, fueled by a combination of economic, political, and social factors. The transfer of the royal court to Brazil had inadvertently accelerated the drive for independence by strengthening Brazilian national consciousness and laying the groundwork for a distinct Brazilian political identity separate from Portugal.

In conclusion, the transfer of the royal court to Brazil and the subsequent independence of Brazil were pivotal events in the history of both nations. These events not only reshaped the political landscape of Portugal and Brazil but also set the stage for a new chapter in Brazilian history as an independent nation. The legacy of this period continues to resonate in the shared cultural heritage and historical ties between Portugal and Brazil, underscoring the interconnected nature of their histories.

Chapter 9

The 19th Century: Turmoil and Change

Political instability and the Liberal Wars

Political instability and the Liberal Wars in 19th-century Portugal were pivotal moments in the country's history, shaping its trajectory towards modernization and constitutional monarchy. This period was marked by social, economic, and political turmoil as competing factions vied for power and influence, leading to a series of conflicts known as the Liberal Wars.

The roots of political instability in Portugal can be traced back to the Napoleonic Wars and the subsequent Peninsular War, which had a profound impact on the country's political landscape. The French invasion of Portugal in 1807 and the subsequent transfer of the royal court to Brazil destabilized the traditional power structures in the country, creating a power vacuum that various factions sought to fill.

In the aftermath of the Napoleonic Wars, tensions between absolutist supporters of the monarchy and liberal reformers advocating for constitutional monarchy came to a head. The reign of King Miguel I, who sought to restore absolutism and roll back liberal reforms, exacerbated these tensions and ultimately led to the outbreak of the Liberal Wars in 1828.

The Liberal Wars were a series of conflicts fought between Miguelist forces, loyal to King Miguel I, and liberal forces supporting the constitutional monarchy established by the liberal revolution of 1820. The conflict was characterized by fierce battles, political intrigue, and shifting alliances as both sides sought to gain the upper hand.

One of the key figures in the Liberal Wars was Dom Pedro, the liberal-minded son of King John VI, who had served as regent of Brazil during his father's exile. Dom Pedro's support for the liberal cause and his willingness to challenge his brother Miguel's claim to the throne played a crucial role in the outcome of the conflict.

The Liberal Wars culminated in the decisive victory of the liberal forces in 1834, with the signing of the Convention of Evoramonte and the exile of King Miguel I. This marked the triumph of the liberal cause and the establishment of a constitutional monarchy in Portugal, ushering in a period of political stability and reform.

The aftermath of the Liberal Wars saw the promulgation of the Constitutional Charter of 1826, which established the framework for a constitutional monarchy in Portugal. The new political order sought to balance the powers of the monarchy with those of the parliament, paving the way for greater political participation and representation.

Overall, the period of political instability and the Liberal Wars in 19th-century Portugal played a crucial role in shaping the country's modern political system and laying the foundations for the establishment of a constitutional monarchy. These events marked a significant step towards democratization and political reform in Portugal, setting the stage for the country's continued development and evolution in the years to come.

The establishment of a constitutional monarchy

The 19th century was a period of significant turmoil and change for Portugal, marked by political instability, social upheaval, and economic challenges. One of the key developments during this time was the establishment of a constitutional monarchy, which played a crucial role in shaping the country's political landscape and paving the way for modernization.

In the early 19th century, Portugal was facing internal strife and external pressures, including the Napoleonic Wars and the invasion of the French forces. This period of instability culminated in the Liberal Wars, a series of conflicts between liberal and absolutist factions vying for control of the government. The outcome of these wars led to the establishment of a constitutional monarchy in Portugal.

The constitutional monarchy was a significant departure from the absolute rule of the monarchy that had characterized Portugal for centuries. Under the new system, the monarch's powers were limited by a constitution that outlined the rights and responsibilities of the government and its citizens. The constitution also established a representative government with a bicameral parliament, where elected representatives had a say in the country's governance.

The establishment of a constitutional monarchy brought about a period of political reforms and modernization efforts in Portugal. The new system aimed to create a more stable and accountable government, promote the rule of law, and protect the rights of the people. It also paved the way for social and economic changes that would shape the country's future trajectory.

One of the key figures in the transition to a constitutional monarchy was King Pedro IV, who played a crucial role in the Liberal Wars and the drafting of the first Portuguese constitution. His efforts to modernize the country and promote liberal reforms were instrumental in laying the foundation for a more democratic and progressive Portugal.

The establishment of a constitutional monarchy also had broader implications for Portuguese society and its relationship with other European nations. Portugal's shift towards a more representative form of government aligned it with the political trends of the time, as other countries in Europe were also transitioning towards constitutional monarchies and parliamentary systems.

Overall, the establishment of a constitutional monarchy in the 19th century marked a significant turning point in Portugal's history. It set the stage for further political, social, and economic reforms that would shape the country's development in the years to come. The transition to a constitutional monarchy helped Portugal navigate the challenges of the 19th century and laid the groundwork for its evolution into a modern nation with a democratic government.

Economic and social changes in 19th century Portugal
In the 19th century, Portugal underwent significant economic and social changes that shaped the course of its history. This period was marked by political turmoil, economic challenges, and social transformations that set the stage for the modernization and development of the country.

Economically, Portugal faced a series of challenges during the 19th century that had a profound impact on its society. The country experienced economic instability, largely due to its reliance on agriculture and trade. Portugal's economy was heavily dependent on exporting agricultural products such as wine, cork, and olive oil, which made it vulnerable to fluctuations in international markets.

The Napoleonic Wars and the subsequent Peninsular War further exacerbated Portugal's economic woes. The wars disrupted trade and commerce, leading to a decline in economic activity and widespread poverty. The country struggled to recover from the devastation caused by the wars, leading to a period of economic stagnation and hardship for many Portuguese people.

In response to these challenges, the Portuguese government implemented a series of economic reforms aimed at modernizing the country's economy. The Marquis of Pombal, in particular, played a key role in promoting economic development through his Pombaline reforms. These reforms focused on promoting industry, improving infrastructure, and expanding trade, with the goal of stimulating economic growth and reducing Portugal's dependence on agriculture.

One of the most significant economic developments of the 19th century was the establishment of a constitutional monarchy in Portugal. The adoption of a constitution in 1820 marked a turning point in the country's history, as it paved the way for political and economic reforms that aimed to modernize the Portuguese state and society.

Socially, the 19th century was also a period of profound change in Portugal. The country experienced rapid urbanization and industrialization, leading to the growth of cities and the emergence of a new urban middle class. The rise of industrial capitalism and the expansion of trade and commerce transformed Portuguese society, creating new opportunities for social mobility and economic advancement.

At the same time, the 19th century also saw the emergence of social movements and political activism in Portugal. The Liberal Wars, which were fought between absolutist and liberal forces, reflected the growing political consciousness and demands for reform among the Portuguese population. The establishment of a constitutional monarchy in 1834 represented a significant victory for the liberal movement and marked the beginning of a new era of political development in Portugal.

Overall, the 19th century was a period of profound change and transformation for Portugal. The country faced economic challenges, political upheaval, and social unrest, but also experienced significant progress in terms of modernization and development. The economic and social changes of the 19th century set the stage for Portugal's continued evolution as a modern European nation and shaped its path towards the future.

Chapter 10

The First Republic

The fall of the monarchy and the establishment of the Portuguese Republic in 1910

The fall of the monarchy and the establishment of the Portuguese Republic in 1910 marked a significant turning point in Portugal's history, ushering in a new era of political change and modernization. This period was characterized by political upheaval, social unrest, and a growing desire for reform and democratization.

The late 19th and early 20th centuries saw Portugal facing numerous challenges, including economic instability, social inequality, and political corruption. The monarchy, led by King Manuel II, was increasingly seen as outdated and out of touch with the needs and aspirations of the Portuguese people. Dissatisfaction with the monarchy grew among various sectors of society, including intellectuals, liberals, and republicans who called for political reform and the establishment of a more democratic system of government.

The roots of the republican movement in Portugal can be traced back to the mid-19th century, with various uprisings and attempts to overthrow the monarchy. However, it was not until the early 20th century that the republican movement gained significant momentum. The Portuguese Republican Party, founded in 1903, became a major force in challenging the monarchy and advocating for a republican form of government based on democratic principles and social justice.

The turning point came on October 5, 1910, when a successful republican revolution led to the overthrow of King Manuel II and the establishment of the Portuguese Republic. The revolution was marked by widespread popular support, with urban workers, intellectuals, and military officers joining forces to bring an end to the monarchy. The revolution was relatively peaceful, with minimal violence and bloodshed compared to other revolutionary movements of the time.

Following the establishment of the republic, a provisional government was formed to oversee the transition to a new political system. A new republican constitution was drafted, which enshrined principles such as universal suffrage, separation of powers, and the protection of individual rights and freedoms. The monarchy was officially abolished, and Portugal became a republic for the first time in its history.

The establishment of the Portuguese Republic in 1910 was met with both hope and challenges. While many saw it as a step towards progress and modernization, the new republic faced immediate difficulties, including political instability, economic turmoil, and social unrest. The transition from a monarchy to a republic was not without its obstacles, as different factions within the republican movement vied for power and influence.

In conclusion, the fall of the monarchy and the establishment of the Portuguese Republic in 1910 marked a pivotal moment in Portugal's history, symbolizing a shift towards democracy and social change. The events of 1910 laid the foundation for a new era of political development and societal transformation, shaping the course of Portuguese history in the decades to come.

Political upheaval and the challenges of the First Republic

The establishment of the Portuguese Republic in 1910 marked a significant turning point in Portugal's history, ushering in a period of political upheaval and challenges as the country grappled with the transition from a monarchy to a republic. The fall of the monarchy was accompanied by a wave of optimism and enthusiasm for democratic reforms and modernization, but the early years of the First Republic were marked by instability, factionalism, and social unrest.

One of the key challenges faced by the First Republic was the deep-seated divisions within Portuguese society. The republican movement itself was a broad coalition of different groups with varying political ideologies, ranging from liberal democrats to radical socialists and anarchists. This diversity of perspectives often led to internal conflicts and power struggles, making it difficult to establish a unified and coherent government.

The new republican government also faced resistance from conservative forces, including monarchists, the Catholic Church, and the military. These groups were deeply entrenched in Portuguese society and were skeptical of the republican government's ability to govern effectively and maintain order. Their opposition often manifested in political conspiracies, attempted coups, and violent uprisings, further destabilizing the fragile republic.

Economic challenges also plagued the First Republic, as Portugal struggled to modernize its economy and address social inequality. The country faced high levels of poverty, illiteracy, and rural underdevelopment, while industrialization and urbanization proceeded at a slow pace. The government's attempts to implement land reforms, improve education, and promote industrial growth were hampered by limited resources, bureaucratic inefficiency, and resistance from entrenched interests.

The First Republic's foreign policy was another source of contention and instability. Portugal's colonial empire was in decline, as nationalist movements in Africa and Asia agitated for independence, while international rivals like Britain and Germany challenged Portuguese territorial claims. The republic's efforts to assert its influence abroad often led to diplomatic crises and military conflicts, further straining its already fragile domestic situation.

Despite these challenges, the First Republic did achieve some notable successes. It established a new constitution that enshrined civil liberties, universal suffrage, and secularism, laying the foundation for a more democratic and inclusive society. The republic also made strides in education, healthcare, and social welfare, improving the lives of many Portuguese citizens.

In conclusion, the First Republic of Portugal was a period of political upheaval and challenges, characterized by internal divisions, social unrest, economic struggles, and foreign conflicts. While the republic made significant strides in advancing democratic principles and social reforms, its inability to effectively address the country's deep-seated problems ultimately led to its downfall and the subsequent rise of authoritarian regimes.

Portugal's role in World War I
During World War I, Portugal played a crucial role as a member of the Allied Powers. Although the country initially declared its neutrality in the conflict, it eventually joined the war on the side

of the Allies in 1916. Portugal's involvement in World War I had significant political, economic, and social implications for the country.

Portugal's decision to enter the war was influenced by several factors. One key reason was the longstanding alliance with Britain, dating back to the Treaty of Windsor in 1386. Portugal's government saw an opportunity to strengthen its ties with Britain and safeguard its colonial interests by supporting the Allies in the war effort.

Portugal's participation in World War I had a direct impact on its African colonies, particularly in Angola and Mozambique. German forces launched incursions into these territories, prompting Portugal to mobilize its military to defend its overseas possessions. The Portuguese colonial troops played a vital role in securing these territories and supporting the Allied war effort in Africa.

On the European front, Portugal sent an expeditionary force to fight in the Western Front alongside British and French troops. The Portuguese soldiers faced challenging conditions and suffered heavy casualties during their participation in the war. Despite these hardships, the Portuguese military made significant contributions to the Allied cause, particularly in the Battle of La Lys in 1918.

Portugal's involvement in World War I also had economic repercussions for the country. The war strained Portugal's resources and led to economic difficulties, including inflation and shortages of essential goods. The government implemented measures to address these challenges, such as rationing and price controls, to mitigate the impact of the war on the civilian population.

Socially, World War I had a profound effect on Portuguese society. The war experience exposed many soldiers to the harsh realities of combat and the trauma of warfare. The sacrifices made by Portuguese soldiers on the battlefield were recognized and honored by the nation, contributing to a sense of national pride and solidarity.

Overall, Portugal's role in World War I was a transformative period in the country's history. The war tested Portugal's military capabilities, strained its resources, and reshaped its relationships with other European powers. Despite the challenges and sacrifices, Portugal's participation in the conflict demonstrated its commitment to its allies and its willingness to defend its interests on the global stage.

Chapter 11

The Estado Novo Regime

Rise of António de Oliveira Salazar & the Estado Novo regime
The rise of António de Oliveira Salazar and the Estado Novo regime marked a significant chapter in the history of Portugal, shaping the country's political landscape and society for several decades. Salazar, a conservative economist and academic, came to power in 1932 during a period of economic turmoil and political instability in Portugal. His authoritarian rule and the establishment of the Estado Novo (New State) regime aimed to restore order, stability, and traditional values in the country.

Salazar's regime was characterized by a centralized and authoritarian government, with a strong emphasis on conservative Catholic values, nationalism, and anti-communism. The Estado Novo regime sought to maintain control over all aspects of Portuguese society, including politics, the economy, and culture. Salazar implemented a corporatist system that favored big business, landowners, and the Catholic Church, while suppressing dissent and political opposition.

Under Salazar's leadership, Portugal experienced a period of economic stability and modernization, with a focus on agricultural and industrial development, infrastructure projects, and social welfare programs. Salazar's policies also emphasized self-sufficiency and protectionism, limiting foreign influence and trade in order to strengthen the Portuguese economy.

However, the Estado Novo regime was also marked by political repression, censorship, and a lack of democratic freedoms. Salazar maintained a tight grip on power through a network of secret police and informants, silencing dissent and opposition through intimidation and imprisonment. The regime's control extended to all aspects of public life, including education, media, and cultural expression.

Internationally, Salazar's Portugal maintained close ties with other authoritarian regimes, including Franco's Spain and Nazi Germany, while remaining neutral during World War II. Portugal's colonial empire in Africa and Asia also played a significant role in Salazar's foreign policy, as he sought to maintain and expand Portuguese influence overseas.

The Estado Novo regime faced increasing challenges and criticisms in the 1960s and 1970s, as social and political pressures mounted both domestically and internationally. Economic stagnation, social inequality, and growing demands for political reform led to widespread protests and unrest, culminating in the Carnation Revolution of 1974.

The Carnation Revolution marked the end of Salazar's authoritarian rule and the Estado Novo regime, paving the way for Portugal's transition to democracy. Salazar's legacy continues to be a subject of debate and controversy in Portugal, with some viewing him as a stern but effective leader who brought stability and modernization to the country, while others criticize his repressive policies and human rights abuses.

In conclusion, the rise of António de Oliveira Salazar and the Estado Novo regime represented a complex and controversial period in Portugal's history, characterized by authoritarian rule, economic development, and political repression. Salazar's legacy continues to shape Portugal's national identity and political landscape, underscoring the enduring impact of his leadership on the country's historical journey.

Economic policies and social changes under the dictatorship
During the period of the Estado Novo regime in Portugal, which was led by António de Oliveira Salazar, the economic policies and social changes implemented had profound impacts on the country. Salazar's regime, which lasted from 1933 to 1974, aimed to establish a corporatist authoritarian state that controlled all aspects of society, including the economy.

Economic Policies:
Under Salazar's rule, the economic policies of the Estado Novo regime were characterized by a strong emphasis on autarky, or economic self-sufficiency. The regime sought to reduce Portugal's dependence on foreign imports and promote domestic production. This was achieved through the implementation of protectionist measures such as high tariffs on imported goods and strict controls on foreign exchange.

Salazar's government also focused on promoting agricultural and industrial development within Portugal. The regime invested heavily in infrastructure projects such as road construction, port development, and hydroelectric power plants to stimulate economic growth. State-owned enterprises were established in key industries such as banking, telecommunications, and transportation, further consolidating the government's control over the economy.

Additionally, the Estado Novo regime implemented policies to control inflation and stabilize the currency. The regime maintained a tight grip on fiscal policy, keeping government spending in check and avoiding excessive borrowing. This conservative approach to economic management helped Portugal avoid the hyperinflation and economic instability experienced by other European countries during the same period.

Social Changes:
In addition to its economic policies, the Estado Novo regime also implemented significant social changes aimed at promoting traditional values and social cohesion. The regime emphasized the importance of family, religion, and patriotism, and sought to maintain social order and discipline through strict censorship and control of public discourse.

The regime also promoted a hierarchical social structure, with a focus on preserving the privileges of the elite and limiting the rights of the working class. Labor unions were tightly controlled by the government, and strikes and protests were heavily suppressed. The regime also enforced strict censorship of the media and cultural institutions, limiting freedom of expression and promoting a conservative social agenda.

Despite the economic development achieved under the Estado Novo regime, there were significant social costs associated with its policies. The regime's emphasis on traditional values and authoritarian control stifled political dissent and limited individual freedoms. Many Portuguese citizens lived in poverty, especially in rural areas, where access to education and healthcare was limited.

In conclusion, the economic policies and social changes implemented under the Estado Novo regime in Portugal had complex and far-reaching consequences. While the regime succeeded in promoting economic development and stability, it also perpetuated social inequalities and restricted individual freedoms. The legacy of the Estado Novo continues to shape Portugal's society and economy to this day, serving as a reminder of the challenges and complexities of authoritarian rule.

Portugal's Role in World War II and the Cold War:

World War II:
During World War II, Portugal maintained a policy of neutrality, aiming to protect its sovereignty and avoid entanglement in the conflict. This stance was influenced by the country's recent experience during the Spanish Civil War and the desire to preserve its colonial empire. However, despite its official neutrality, Portugal played a significant role in supporting both the Allies and the Axis powers.

Portugal's geographic location on the western edge of Europe made it a strategic point for both sides. The country provided valuable intelligence to the Allies, particularly in monitoring German U-boat activity in the Atlantic Ocean. The Azores, a group of islands under Portuguese control, also served as an important base for Allied operations, including air and naval support.

Economically, Portugal maintained trade relations with both sides during the war. The country benefited from exporting goods to Allied countries, such as tungsten and cork, while also supplying resources to Axis powers like Germany. This delicate balancing act allowed Portugal to benefit economically without fully committing to either side.

In 1943, as the tide of the war began to turn in favor of the Allies, Portugal signed the Luso-British Agreement, allowing the Allies to establish military bases in the Azores in exchange for economic and military aid. This agreement further solidified Portugal's support for the Allied cause without officially entering the war.

Cold War:

After World War II, Portugal found itself in a challenging position as the world entered the era of the Cold War. The country's authoritarian Estado Novo regime, led by António de Oliveira Salazar, aligned itself with the Western bloc, particularly the United States. This alignment was driven by Portugal's desire to maintain its colonial empire and protect its interests in Africa and Asia.

Portugal's support for the Western bloc led to its participation in various Cold War initiatives, including joining the North Atlantic Treaty Organization (NATO) in 1949. Portugal's membership in NATO allowed for increased military cooperation with Western powers and further solidified its position as a key player in Cold War geopolitics.

The Cold War also had significant implications for Portugal's colonial holdings, particularly in Africa. The pro-independence movements in Portuguese colonies, such as Angola, Mozambique, and Guinea-Bissau, became battlegrounds for Cold War rivalries. Portugal's efforts to suppress these movements were supported by Western powers, while communist countries like the Soviet Union backed the independence fighters.

In 1974, the Carnation Revolution in Portugal led to the end of the Estado Novo regime and marked a turning point in the country's Cold War policies. The new democratic government initiated decolonization processes, leading to the eventual independence of Portugal's African colonies. This shift in policy reflected the changing dynamics of the Cold War and Portugal's evolving role in the international arena.

Overall, Portugal's role in World War II and the Cold War was characterized by a delicate balancing act between neutrality and alignment with Western powers. The country's strategic location, economic interests, and colonial holdings shaped its decisions during these tumultuous periods, ultimately influencing its trajectory in the post-war era.

Chapter 12

The Carnation Revolution and Modern Portugal

The Decline of the Estado Novo and the Colonial Wars

The Estado Novo regime in Portugal, led by António de Oliveira Salazar, faced increasing challenges in the mid-20th century that ultimately led to its decline. One of the key factors that contributed to the regime's downfall was its involvement in colonial wars in Africa, particularly in Angola, Mozambique, and Guinea-Bissau.

The colonial wars began in the early 1960s as nationalist movements in Portugal's African colonies sought independence from colonial rule. The Portuguese government, under the Estado Novo regime, responded with a heavy-handed military approach to suppress these movements. The wars were prolonged and brutal, resulting in significant loss of life on both sides and drawing international condemnation.

As the colonial wars dragged on, Portugal faced mounting economic and social challenges. The cost of maintaining the military presence in Africa strained the country's resources, leading to economic stagnation and increasing poverty at home. The international community, including Portugal's NATO allies, began to pressure the regime to end its colonial policies and grant independence to its African colonies.

Internally, opposition to the Estado Novo regime grew as people became disillusioned with its repressive policies and the prolonged conflicts in Africa. The regime's authoritarian rule and censorship of dissenting voices further fueled public discontent and calls for change.

In 1974, a group of military officers staged a coup known as the Carnation Revolution, which aimed to overthrow the Estado Novo regime and bring about democratic reforms. The revolution was largely peaceful, marked by the widespread distribution of carnations to symbolize non-violence and hope for a new beginning.

The Carnation Revolution spelled the end of the Estado Novo regime and ushered in a period of political transition and democratization in Portugal. The new democratic government, led by civilian and military figures, initiated a process of decolonization, granting independence to Angola, Mozambique, Cape Verde, Guinea-Bissau, and São Tomé and Príncipe.

The legacy of the colonial wars and the decline of the Estado Novo regime had a lasting impact on Portugal's national identity and foreign relations. The country underwent a period of introspection and reconciliation as it came to terms with its colonial past and sought to forge new relationships with its former colonies.

In conclusion, the decline of the Estado Novo regime and the colonial wars marked a significant turning point in Portugal's history, leading to the end of authoritarian rule and the beginning of a new era of democracy and independence. The events of this period continue to shape Portugal's national identity and its relationships with its former colonies in Africa.

Carnation Revolution of 1974 & the transition to democracy

The Carnation Revolution of 1974 stands as a pivotal moment in Portuguese history, marking the end of nearly five decades of authoritarian rule under the Estado Novo regime. This revolution, also known as the 25th of April Revolution, was a largely peaceful military coup that took place on April 25, 1974, in Lisbon, Portugal. It was named after the red carnations that were placed in the muzzles of rifles by the military and civilians as a symbol of non-violent resistance.

The Carnation Revolution was a response to the oppressive policies of the Estado Novo regime, led by Prime Minister António de Oliveira Salazar and later Marcelo Caetano. The regime had maintained tight control over political dissent, civil liberties, and economic development, leading to widespread social unrest and dissatisfaction among the Portuguese population. The revolution was fueled by a desire for freedom, democracy, and social justice.

The catalyst for the revolution was the military dissatisfaction with the ongoing colonial wars in Africa, particularly in Angola, Mozambique, and Guinea-Bissau. The military, led by a group of young officers known as the Armed Forces Movement (MFA), initiated the coup by seizing key strategic points in Lisbon without the use of violence. The population, tired of the regime's repressive policies and the costly colonial wars, quickly joined the movement, resulting in a bloodless transition of power.

The Carnation Revolution led to the downfall of the Estado Novo regime and the establishment of a democratic government in Portugal. Following the revolution, a transitional military government was formed, known as the National Salvation Junta, which initiated a process of political reform and democratization.

The new government immediately began dismantling the authoritarian structures of the old regime, including censorship, political repression, and restrictions on civil liberties.

One of the most significant outcomes of the Carnation Revolution was the drafting and approval of a new democratic constitution in 1976. The Constitution of the Portuguese Republic established Portugal as a democratic state based on the principles of freedom, equality, and social justice. It enshrined fundamental rights and freedoms, established a system of checks and balances, and outlined the framework for a multi-party political system and regular elections.

The Carnation Revolution also had profound social and cultural implications for Portugal. It paved the way for a period of social and cultural liberalization, allowing for the expression of diverse political opinions and the flourishing of artistic and intellectual creativity. The revolution brought about a sense of national unity and pride, as the Portuguese people came together to shape their own destiny and build a democratic society based on shared values and aspirations.

In conclusion, the Carnation Revolution of 1974 was a transformative event in Portuguese history that marked the transition from dictatorship to democracy. It symbolized the triumph of freedom over oppression, unity over division, and hope over despair. The legacy of the revolution continues to shape Portugal's national identity and serves as a reminder of the power of ordinary people to effect positive change through peaceful means.

Decolonization and the end of the Portuguese Empire

Decolonization and the end of the Portuguese Empire marked a significant turning point in Portugal's history, shaping its identity and relationships with its former colonies. This chapter delves into the complex process of decolonization and its impact on Portugal and its overseas territories.

The decolonization of the Portuguese Empire was a prolonged and tumultuous process that unfolded over several decades, marked by both peaceful transitions and violent conflicts. Portugal's colonial holdings in Africa, Asia, and the Americas had been a source of wealth and power for centuries, but by the mid-20th century, pressures for independence were mounting both internally and externally.

In Africa, Portugal faced fierce resistance from nationalist movements in its colonies of Angola, Mozambique, Guinea-Bissau, Cape Verde, and São Tomé and Príncipe. The African colonies had long been subjected to oppressive colonial rule and exploitation, leading to widespread poverty, inequality, and social unrest. The African independence movements, such as the MPLA in Angola and FRELIMO in Mozambique, waged armed struggles for self-determination, challenging Portugal's authority and control.

The Portuguese government, under the authoritarian Estado Novo regime led by António de Oliveira Salazar, initially resisted granting independence to its colonies, viewing them as integral parts of the Portuguese nation. However, international pressure and internal dissent forced Portugal to reconsider its colonial policies. The Carnation Revolution of 1974, a peaceful military coup supported by civilians, brought an end to the Estado Novo regime and paved the way for a democratic transition.

Following the Carnation Revolution, Portugal embarked on a process of decolonization, negotiating independence with its African colonies. The newly formed government under the leadership of the Socialist Party sought to disengage from its colonial past and forge new relationships based on cooperation and mutual respect. The independence of Angola, Mozambique, Cape Verde, Guinea-Bissau, and São Tomé and Príncipe was achieved through diplomatic agreements and peace accords, although not without some violence and instability.

Decolonization had profound consequences for Portugal, both politically and economically. The loss of its overseas territories meant the end of the Portuguese Empire and a redefinition of Portugal's national identity. The country experienced a period of introspection and soul-searching, grappling with the legacy of colonialism and its impact on its former colonies. The process of decolonization also brought about economic challenges, as Portugal had to adapt to a new reality without the resources and markets provided by its colonies.

In conclusion, the decolonization of the Portuguese Empire was a complex and transformative chapter in Portugal's history. It reflected the changing dynamics of the post-colonial world and the aspirations of formerly colonized peoples for self-determination and independence. Decolonization marked the end of an era for Portugal and the beginning of a new chapter in its relationship with its former colonies, characterized by efforts to reconcile the past, promote dialogue, and build a more inclusive and equitable future for all involved.

Chapter 13

Contemporary Portugal

Portugal's integration into the European Union

Portugal's integration into the European Union marked a significant chapter in its history, shaping its economy, politics, and society in the late 20th and early 21st centuries. The decision to join the European Economic Community (EEC) in 1986 was a crucial step towards modernizing and aligning Portugal with its European neighbors. This move not only opened up new opportunities for trade and investment but also signaled Portugal's commitment to democratic values and European integration.

One of the key aspects of Portugal's integration into the European Union was its impact on the country's economy. Access to the EU's single market provided Portuguese businesses with a larger consumer base and facilitated trade with other member states. Structural funds and investment from the EU also played a vital role in modernizing Portugal's infrastructure, promoting regional development, and boosting economic growth. The adoption of the euro as the national currency in 1999 further strengthened Portugal's economic ties with the EU and facilitated trade and financial transactions within the Eurozone.

In addition to economic benefits, EU membership brought about significant political changes in Portugal. As a member of the European Union, Portugal had to align its policies and legislation with EU standards and regulations. This process of harmonization led to reforms in various sectors, including agriculture, fisheries, and environmental protection, to meet EU requirements. Furthermore, Portugal's participation in EU decision-making bodies and institutions allowed it to have a say in shaping EU policies and initiatives that directly impacted its national interests.

The social and cultural impact of Portugal's integration into the European Union was also profound. Increased mobility within the EU facilitated greater exchange of people, ideas, and cultures, enriching Portugal's cultural landscape and promoting cross-border cooperation. EU programs such as Erasmus+ fostered educational exchanges and collaborations, enabling Portuguese students and professionals to gain international experience and broaden their horizons. Furthermore, EU initiatives promoting social cohesion and inclusion helped address social inequalities and promote sustainable development in Portugal.

Portugal's integration into the European Union also had implications for its national identity and sovereignty. While EU membership brought numerous benefits, it also required Portugal to cede some degree of autonomy in decision-making to EU institutions. Debates over issues such as sovereignty, national identity, and the balance of power between the EU and its member states continued to shape public discourse and political debates in Portugal.

In conclusion, Portugal's integration into the European Union has been a transformative journey that has reshaped the country's economy, politics, and society. By embracing European values and principles, Portugal has strengthened its position within the European community and contributed to the broader project of

European integration. As Portugal continues to navigate the complexities of EU membership, it remains an active participant in shaping the future of Europe and realizing its potential as a modern, dynamic, and globally connected nation.

Economic development and challenges in the late 20th and early 21st centuries

In the late 20th and early 21st centuries, Portugal experienced significant economic development and faced various challenges that shaped its modern economic landscape. Following the Carnation Revolution of 1974 and the transition to democracy, Portugal embarked on a path of economic modernization and integration into the European Union, which brought about both opportunities and obstacles.

One of the key drivers of economic development in this period was Portugal's accession to the European Economic Community (EEC) in 1986, which later evolved into the European Union (EU). Membership in the EU facilitated increased trade, investment, and access to funding for infrastructure projects, leading to a period of economic growth and convergence with wealthier European nations. Structural funds provided by the EU supported the development of Portugal's infrastructure, education system, and technological capabilities, contributing to improved productivity and competitiveness.

However, despite these positive developments, Portugal also faced several challenges that impacted its economic performance. One of the major challenges was the issue of economic disparities between the more developed coastal regions and the poorer interior regions, leading to regional inequalities and social imbalances. The economic crisis of the late 2000s, triggered by the global financial crisis, exposed Portugal's vulnerabilities, including high public debt, low productivity growth, and a reliance on external borrowing.

The economic downturn of the late 2000s and early 2010s resulted in a severe recession, with high unemployment rates, austerity measures, and a contraction in domestic demand. Portugal was forced to implement structural reforms, including fiscal consolidation, labor market reforms, and privatization of state-owned enterprises, to stabilize its economy and meet the conditions of the EU-IMF bailout program.

Despite these challenges, Portugal gradually recovered from the economic crisis and implemented measures to enhance its economic resilience and competitiveness. The country diversified its export base, focusing on high-value-added sectors such as tourism, renewable energy, and information technology. Investments in innovation, research, and development aimed to enhance Portugal's technological capabilities and foster entrepreneurship and innovation.

Moreover, Portugal's economic development in the late 20th and early 21st centuries was also influenced by globalization trends, digitalization, and demographic shifts. The rise of the knowledge-based economy, the digital transformation of industries, and the need for skilled labor posed both opportunities and challenges for Portugal's economic development. The aging population and emigration of skilled workers also posed demographic challenges that required long-term planning and policy interventions.

In conclusion, Portugal's economic journey in the late 20th and early 21st centuries reflects a complex interplay of opportunities and challenges that have shaped its modern economic landscape. The country's integration into the EU, structural reforms, and investments in innovation and competitiveness have positioned Portugal as a dynamic and resilient economy in the global context, while also highlighting the need for continued efforts to address regional disparities, promote sustainable development, and ensure inclusive growth for all segments of society.

Cultural renaissance and contributions to global culture
Portugal has a rich cultural heritage that has made significant contributions to global culture throughout its history. The cultural renaissance in Portugal refers to a period of revival and flourishing of arts, literature, music, and architecture that occurred during various periods in the nation's history. These cultural achievements have left a lasting impact on the world and have helped shape Portugal's national identity.

One of the most notable aspects of Portugal's cultural renaissance is its literature. Portuguese literature has a long and illustrious history, dating back to the Middle Ages with epic poems such as "The Lusiads" by Luís de Camões, which celebrates the nation's maritime discoveries and explores themes of heroism, exploration, and national identity. In the modern era, Portuguese literature has continued to thrive with the works of renowned authors such as José Saramago, who won the Nobel Prize in Literature in 1998 for his novel "Blindness."

Portugal's contributions to music have also been significant. Fado, a traditional Portuguese music genre characterized by mournful melodies and poetic lyrics, has captured the hearts of people around the world. Artists like Amália Rodrigues and Mariza have helped popularize Fado internationally, showcasing the emotional depth and cultural richness of Portuguese music.

Portuguese architecture is another aspect of the nation's cultural renaissance that has garnered global recognition. From the Manueline style of the 16th century, characterized by intricate decorations and maritime motifs, to the Pombaline architecture of the 18th century, known for its earthquake-resistant design, Portugal's architectural heritage is diverse and influential. The historic city of Lisbon, with its charming neighborhoods, grand palaces, and picturesque streets, stands as a testament to Portugal's architectural legacy.

In the realm of visual arts, Portuguese artists have made significant contributions to global culture. The works of painters like Nuno Gonçalves, José Malhoa, and Paula Rego have gained international acclaim for their unique styles and thematic explorations. Portuguese artists have drawn inspiration from their country's history, landscapes, and traditions, creating art that reflects the nation's cultural richness and diversity.

Portugal's cultural renaissance has also extended to the field of cinema, with Portuguese filmmakers making a mark on the international stage. Directors like Manoel de Oliveira, Pedro Costa, and Miguel Gomes have garnered critical acclaim for their innovative storytelling and cinematic achievements, contributing to the global film industry and showcasing Portugal's talent and creativity.

Overall, Portugal's cultural renaissance and contributions to global culture have been diverse, vibrant, and enduring. From literature and music to architecture and visual arts, Portugal's cultural heritage continues to inspire and captivate audiences around the world. By celebrating its rich cultural legacy and embracing modern innovations, Portugal remains a cultural powerhouse with a unique voice in the global cultural landscape.

Conclusion

Summary of Portugal's historical journey & its global impact
Portugal's historical journey is a rich tapestry woven with conquests, discoveries, and cultural achievements that have left a lasting impact on the world stage. From its ancient roots to its modern-day status as a member of the European Union, Portugal's history is a testament to resilience, innovation, and adaptability.

The early chapters of Portugal's history saw the influence of various civilizations, from the Phoenicians and Greeks to the Romans and Visigoths. The Islamic period brought cultural and economic developments under Moorish rule, setting the stage for the Christian Reconquista and the emergence of Portuguese identity. The birth of Portugal as an independent kingdom marked a turning point, leading to the Age of Expansion and the establishment of a vast empire spanning Africa, Asia, and the Americas.

During the Golden Age of Portugal, the nation reached the zenith of its power and wealth, making significant contributions to science, culture, and trade. The spice trade and colonial enterprises fueled Portugal's prosperity and global influence, shaping the course of world history. The Iberian Union and the subsequent restoration of Portuguese independence highlighted the nation's resilience in the face of dynastic challenges and foreign domination.

The Enlightenment and Reform era brought modernization efforts under the Marquis of Pombal, paving the way for political and social transformations in 19th century Portugal. The transition from monarchy to republic heralded a new chapter in Portuguese history, marked by political upheaval, participation in World War I, and the rise of the Estado Novo regime under António de Oliveira Salazar.

The Carnation Revolution of 1974 marked a turning point in Portugal's modern history, leading to the end of the colonial wars and the transition to democracy. Decolonization and the dissolution of the Portuguese Empire reshaped Portugal's global footprint, while its integration into the European Union signaled a new era of economic development and cultural exchange.

In the contemporary era, Portugal continues to navigate the complexities of a changing world, facing economic challenges and embracing cultural renaissance. Its contributions to global culture, from literature and music to art and cuisine, reflect a rich heritage that resonates far beyond its borders. As Portugal looks to the future, its historical journey serves as a source of inspiration and guidance, shaping its national identity and informing its prospects on the world stage.

Through triumphs and tribulations, Portugal's historical narrative embodies the spirit of exploration, innovation, and resilience that have defined its place in world history. As the nation continues to evolve and adapt to a rapidly changing world, its past achievements and enduring legacy serve as a foundation for future growth and prosperity.

Reflections on Portugal's National Identity & Future Prospects
Portugal's historical journey has played a significant role in shaping its national identity and future prospects. Throughout the

centuries, Portugal has faced numerous challenges and changes that have influenced how the country perceives itself and its place in the world. From the early days of ancient Portugal to the modern era, the Portuguese have developed a strong sense of pride in their history, culture, and achievements.

One of the key aspects of Portugal's national identity is its role as a maritime power and a global empire. The Age of Exploration during the 15th and 16th centuries saw Portuguese navigators and explorers like Vasco da Gama and Bartolomeu Dias establish trade routes and colonies in Africa, Asia, and the Americas. This era of expansion brought wealth, prestige, and cultural exchange to Portugal, shaping its identity as a nation with a rich history of exploration and discovery.

The legacy of the Portuguese Empire continues to influence Portugal's national identity today. The country's cultural heritage, including its language, cuisine, and music, reflects the diverse influences of its former colonies and trading partners. The global reach of Portuguese culture has helped to strengthen ties with other countries and promote a sense of unity among Portuguese-speaking nations.

In more recent history, Portugal has undergone significant political and social changes that have shaped its national identity. The Carnation Revolution of 1974 marked the end of the Estado Novo dictatorship and the beginning of a new era of democracy and freedom. This peaceful revolution demonstrated the resilience and determination of the Portuguese people to strive for a better future based on democratic principles and human rights.

As Portugal entered the European Union in 1986, the country's national identity became increasingly intertwined with its European identity. Membership in the EU has brought economic benefits, increased cooperation with other member states, and enhanced Portugal's standing on the world stage. However, challenges such as economic disparities, political instability, and social inequality have also emerged, raising questions about Portugal's place in a rapidly changing global landscape.

Looking towards the future, Portugal faces both opportunities and challenges that will shape its national identity in the 21st century. The country's rich history, cultural heritage, and spirit of exploration provide a strong foundation for continued growth and development. Embracing innovation, sustainability, and diversity will be key to ensuring Portugal's competitiveness and resilience in an increasingly interconnected world.

In conclusion, Portugal's national identity is a reflection of its past achievements, struggles, and aspirations. The country's history as a global empire, its commitment to democracy and human rights, and its role in the European Union all contribute to a sense of pride and unity among the Portuguese people. By embracing its cultural diversity, fostering economic growth, and promoting social inclusion, Portugal can continue to build a bright future that honors its past while embracing new opportunities for progress and prosperity.

Appendices

Timeline of key events in Portuguese history
The timeline of key events in Portuguese history spans millennia and is a testament to the rich and diverse tapestry of the nation's past. From ancient civilizations to modern-day developments, Portugal has undergone numerous significant milestones that have shaped its identity and legacy on the global stage.

1. Prehistoric and Early Human Settlements (Pre-1000 BCE)
- Prehistoric hunter-gatherer societies inhabit the Iberian Peninsula.
- The arrival of Celtic tribes in the region, influencing early Portuguese culture.
- Phoenician traders establish trading posts along the coast, introducing new goods and ideas to the local population.

2. Roman Conquest and Lusitania (2nd century BCE - 5th century CE)
- Roman legions conquer the Iberian Peninsula, leading to the integration of Lusitania into the Roman Empire.
- Romanization of the region, including the construction of roads, bridges, and cities.
- The decline of Roman rule and the arrival of the Visigoths in the 5th century CE.

3. Moorish Invasion and Al-Andalus (8th - 12th centuries)
- The Moors invade the Iberian Peninsula, establishing Al-Andalus in the south.
- Cultural and economic developments flourish under Islamic rule.
- The Christian Reconquista begins, leading to the emergence of Portuguese identity.

4. Birth of Portugal and Independence (12th - 13th centuries)
- The County of Portugal is established, with Count Henry playing a key role in its formation.
- Afonso Henriques declares himself king after the Battle of Ourique in 1139.
- The Treaty of Zamora in 1143 secures Portuguese independence from the Kingdom of León.

5. Age of Exploration and Empire (15th - 16th centuries)
- Prince Henry the Navigator promotes maritime exploration, leading to the discovery of new lands.
- Vasco da Gama's voyage to India in 1498 establishes a sea route to the East.
- The Portuguese Empire expands across Africa, Asia, and the Americas, becoming a global power.

6. Golden Age of Portugal (16th century)
- Portugal reaches the height of its power and wealth during the Age of Discovery.
- Cultural and scientific achievements flourish, with notable figures like Luís de Camões and Fernão Mendes Pinto.
- The spice trade and colonial enterprises contribute to Portugal's prosperity.

7. Iberian Union and Restoration (17th century)
- Portugal enters a dynastic crisis and unites with Spain under the Iberian Union.
- The Portuguese Restoration War in 1640 leads to the end of Spanish rule.
- The Braganza dynasty is established, ushering in a period of rebuilding and stability.

8. Enlightenment and Modernization (18th - 19th centuries)
- The Marquis of Pombal implements reforms to modernize Portugal's economy and society.
- The Napoleonic Wars and Peninsular War impact Portugal, leading to political and social changes.
- The transfer of the royal court to Brazil in 1807 and the independence of Brazil in 1822.

9. 19th Century Turmoil and Change (19th century)
- Political instability and the Liberal Wars shape Portugal's transition to a constitutional monarchy.
- Economic and social changes, including industrialization and urbanization.
- Portugal faces challenges in maintaining its overseas territories and dealing with colonial tensions.

10. First Republic and World War I (20th century)
- The monarchy falls in 1910, and the Portuguese Republic is established.
- Political upheaval and challenges characterize the First Republic era.
- Portugal's involvement in World War I on the side of the Allies.

This timeline of key events in Portuguese history provides a glimpse into the complex and dynamic evolution of a nation that has played a significant role in shaping world history. From ancient civilizations to modern-day developments, Portugal's journey is a testament to resilience, innovation, and cultural richness that continues to inspire and captivate audiences around the globe.

Biographies of notable Portuguese figures:
Portugal has a rich history that has been shaped by numerous influential individuals who have left a lasting impact on the country and the world. From explorers and monarchs to artists and statesmen, Portuguese history is filled with remarkable figures whose contributions have helped shape the course of history. Here are some of the notable Portuguese figures who have played a significant role in shaping the country's past:

1. Prince Henry the Navigator (1394-1460): Known as the driving force behind the Age of Discovery, Prince Henry was a key figure in Portugal's maritime expansion. He established a school of navigation in Sagres, where he sponsored expeditions that led to the discovery of new lands and sea routes. His efforts paved the way for Portuguese explorers like Vasco da Gama and Bartolomeu Dias to chart new territories and establish trade routes with Africa, Asia, and the Americas.

2. Vasco da Gama (1460-1524): A renowned Portuguese explorer, Vasco da Gama is best known for his pioneering voyage to India in 1498. He was the first European to sail directly from Europe to India, opening up a lucrative trade route that would greatly enhance Portugal's wealth and influence. Da Gama's successful expedition solidified Portugal's position as a major player in the Age of Discovery and established the first maritime link between Europe and Asia.

3. Afonso de Albuquerque (1453-1515): A Portuguese nobleman and military commander, Afonso de Albuquerque played a crucial role in expanding Portugal's empire in Asia. Known as the "Great Albuquerque," he conquered strategic ports in the Indian Ocean and established Portuguese control over key trading posts in the region. His aggressive tactics and diplomatic skills helped secure Portugal's dominance in the lucrative spice trade and laid the foundation for the Portuguese Empire in the East.

4. Luís de Camões (1524-1580): Considered Portugal's greatest poet, Luís de Camões is best known for his epic poem "Os Lusíadas," which celebrates Portugal's maritime achievements and explores themes of exploration, heroism, and national identity. His work is regarded as a literary masterpiece and a symbol of Portuguese cultural heritage, earning him a prominent place in the country's literary canon.

5. Marquis of Pombal (1699-1782): Sebastião José de Carvalho e Melo, also known as the Marquis of Pombal, was a statesman and reformer who served as prime minister of Portugal during the reign of King Joseph I. Pombal is credited with modernizing Portugal's economy, infrastructure, and administration through a series of sweeping reforms known as the Pombaline reforms. His policies aimed to strengthen the country's power and prestige, laying the groundwork for Portugal's future development.

6. António de Oliveira Salazar (1889-1970): A prominent figure in 20th-century Portuguese history, António de Oliveira Salazar was a conservative statesman who served as the Prime Minister of Portugal from 1932 to 1968. Known for his authoritarian rule and corporatist policies, Salazar established the Estado Novo regime, which maintained tight control over politics, economy, and society. Despite his controversial legacy, Salazar's influence shaped Portugal's trajectory during a turbulent period of the 20th century.

These notable Portuguese figures represent a diverse array of individuals who have left a lasting legacy on the country's history and culture. Their contributions have helped shape Portugal's identity and influence its place in the world, showcasing the depth and richness of the country's historical heritage.

Glossary of historical terms and names
The glossary of historical terms and names in "The History of Portugal" provides readers with a comprehensive reference guide to key terms, figures, and events mentioned throughout the book. By defining and explaining these terms, the glossary enhances the reader's understanding of Portuguese history and culture. Here is a detailed section on the glossary of historical terms and names:

Afonso Henriques: The first King of Portugal, who played a crucial role in the establishment of the Portuguese nation and its independence from the Kingdom of León.

Al-Andalus: The Islamic state that controlled parts of the Iberian Peninsula, including Portugal, during the medieval period.

Carnation Revolution: A peaceful military coup in Portugal in 1974 that led to the overthrow of the Estado Novo regime and the establishment of democracy.

Count Henry: The father of Afonso Henriques and the first Count of Portugal, whose actions laid the foundation for the independence of Portugal.

Estado Novo: The authoritarian regime in Portugal established by António de Oliveira Salazar in the mid-20th century, characterized by censorship, political repression, and economic austerity.

Marquis of Pombal: Sebastião José de Carvalho e Melo, who served as the prime minister of Portugal in the 18th century and implemented significant reforms to modernize the country.

Phoenicians: Ancient seafaring people from the eastern Mediterranean who established trading outposts in Portugal and other parts of the Iberian Peninsula.

Prince Henry the Navigator: Infante Henry of Portugal, a key figure in the Age of Exploration who sponsored numerous voyages of discovery along the African coast.

Reconquista: The Christian reconquest of the Iberian Peninsula from Muslim rule, a process that played a significant role in shaping the history of Portugal.

Treaty of Zamora: An agreement signed in 1143 between Portugal and the Kingdom of León, recognizing Portuguese independence and establishing the borders of the new kingdom.

Visigoths: A Germanic tribe that ruled parts of the Iberian Peninsula, including Portugal, following the fall of the Western Roman Empire.

Vasco da Gama: A Portuguese explorer who led the first maritime expedition from Europe to India, opening up a sea route to the East and expanding Portugal's influence in Asia.

This glossary provides a brief overview of some of the key terms and names that are essential for understanding the complex and rich history of Portugal as outlined in the book. Readers can refer to this section for clarification and context as they delve deeper into the fascinating story of Portugal's past and its enduring impact on the world.

Bibliography and further reading

The Bibliography and further reading section of 'The History of Portugal' serves as a valuable resource for readers who wish to delve deeper into the historical narrative presented in the book. This section provides a list of primary and secondary sources that were consulted by the author in the research and writing process, as well as additional readings for those interested in exploring specific topics further.

Primary sources are essential in historical research as they offer firsthand accounts of events and perspectives from the time period under study. In the context of Portuguese history, primary sources may include chronicles, letters, legal documents, and other contemporary records. Examples of primary sources relevant to the various chapters of this book could include the writings of Roman historians like Tacitus and Livy for the Roman Lusitania chapter, or the letters and treaties related to the establishment of Portuguese independence in the chapter on the Birth of Portugal.

Secondary sources, on the other hand, provide analysis, interpretation, and synthesis of historical events and trends based on primary sources. These sources help to contextualize and deepen our understanding of the past. For readers looking to expand their knowledge of Portuguese history beyond the scope of this book, the Bibliography and further reading section could include scholarly works by historians specializing in different periods of Portuguese history. For example, works by renowned historians such as A. H. de Oliveira Marques, José Hermano Saraiva, and Harold Livermore could be recommended for their comprehensive studies on various aspects of Portuguese history.

In addition to academic works, the Bibliography and further reading section may also include recommendations for general readers interested in exploring Portuguese history through popular and accessible sources. Biographies of key historical figures like Prince Henry the Navigator or António de Oliveira Salazar, as well as historical novels or documentaries focusing on specific events such as the Age of Discovery or the Carnation Revolution, could offer readers a more engaging and narrative-driven approach to learning about Portugal's past.

Furthermore, the Bibliography and further reading section could highlight online resources, archives, and museums that provide additional information and materials related to Portuguese history. Websites of historical institutions like the National Archive of Torre do Tombo or the Museu Nacional de Arte Antiga in Lisbon, for instance, could offer digital access to primary sources, exhibitions, and educational resources for interested readers.

Overall, the Bibliography and further reading section is a crucial component of 'The History of Portugal' that not only acknowledges the sources used in the book but also serves as a guide for readers seeking to deepen their understanding of Portugal's rich and complex historical journey. By providing a diverse selection of primary and secondary sources, as well as recommendations for further exploration through different mediums, this section enhances the educational value of the book and encourages a more comprehensive engagement with the history of Portugal.

Share Your Thoughts!

Dear Valued Reader,

Thank you for reading our history of Portugal book. This book is brought to you by **Skriuwer**, a group dedicated to creating interesting and easy-to-read content. Our goal is to take you through the rich and vibrant history of Portugal, from its early days to its significant influence on the world.

We hope you enjoyed the stories and important moments we gathered for you. Our aim is to give you a book that not only teaches but also shares the adventure and legacy of Portugal, showing how it developed, explored, and influenced history.

Your journey doesn't have to end now that you've finished the book. We see you as a key part of our community. If you have any comments, questions, or ideas on how we can make this book better or what we should write about next, please reach out to us at **kontakt@skriuwer.com**. Your feedback is very helpful and helps us make better content for you and others.

Did the history keep you interested and help you learn more about Portugal? Please leave a review where you bought the book. Your thoughts not only inspire us but also help other readers find and choose this book.

Thank you for choosing **Skriuwer**. Let's keep exploring the fascinating history of Portugal together.

With Thanks,
The Skriuwer Team

Made in the USA
Middletown, DE
21 July 2024

57796007R00060